How to Use the CD-ROM

System requirements vary depending on what software you download from this CD. Please view all available readme files before installation or prior to startup of installed software included on this CD.

Please see Appendix B in this book for more information.

RECOMMENDED SYSTEM REQUIREMENTS

Designed to work on Windows 95 and Windows NT 4.0.

WINDOWS SYSTEM

Computer: Pentium IBM PC-compatiable
Memory: 16MB of RAM
Platform: Windows 95 or NT 4.0
Hardware: 2X CD-ROM Drive

How to ACTIVATE YOUR WEB SITE

How to
ACTIVATE YOUR WEB SITE

BOB ALGIE

Ziff-Davis Press
An imprint of Macmillan Computer Publishing USA
Emeryville, California

Publisher	Joe Wikert
Associate Publisher	Juliet Langley
Acquisitions Editor	Simon Hayes
Development Editor	Angela Allen
Copy Editor	Margo R. Hill
Technical Reviewer	Scott Arpajian
Proofreader	Joe Sadusky
Cover Illustration and Design	Megan Gandt
Book Design	Dennis Gallagher/Visual Strategies, San Francisco
Page Layout	Janet Piercy
Indexer	Richard Genova

Ziff-Davis Press, ZD Press, the Ziff-Davis Press logo are trademarks or registered trademarks of, and are licensed to Macmillan Computer Publishing USA by Ziff-Davis Publishing Company, New York, New York.

Ziff-Davis Press imprint books are produced on a Macintosh computer system with the following applications: FrameMaker®, Microsoft® Word, QuarkXPress®, Adobe Illustrator®, Adobe Photoshop®, Adobe Streamline™, MacLink®Plus, Aldus® FreeHand™, Collage Plus™.

Ziff-Davis Press, an imprint of
Macmillan Computer Publishing USA
5903 Christie Avenue
Emeryville, CA 94608

ISBN 1-56276-527-2
Manufactured in the United States of America
10 9 8 7 6 5 4 3 2 1

The list of individuals I would like to dedicate this book to is finite but too long to include within these pages. To all those who helped me focus my brain and survive the 1980s, I thank you. You know who you are. Special thanks to my wife, Ann, and my sons, Teague and Corey. They inspire me daily and put up with the odd hours I keep in front of the computer.

TABLE OF CONTENTS

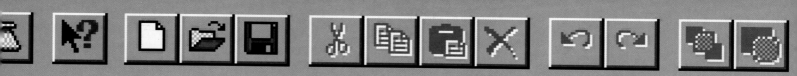

ACKNOWLEDGMENTS

 I would like to thank everyone at Ziff-Davis Press who had a part in putting this book together. Everyone involved deserves some of the credit. In particular, I would like to thank Simon Hayes who stuck with our original idea and got it approved. Thanks too go to Angie Allen, who kept bringing me back to the subject at hand when I got lost or confused, and who had the patience to stick with my quirks. A big thank you to Scott Arpajian who knows more about HTML than I'll ever be able to forget. Thanks also to Margo Hill, Carol Burbo, and Lucresia Ashford, and all the others involved. You're a great team!

INTRODUCTION

How to Activate Your Web Site is a book for beginners and those with a creative mindset who want to publish their own Web pages. It is a good place for anyone to start who has little time or patience for learning new applications and technology. It doesn't assume you have worked with programming languages before. It does assume that you have a little familiarity with the World Wide Web and Windows 95, and that you know your way around enough to lift and depress your index finger and can shove a mouse around on a desktop. It also assumes you wish to take advantage of the marvelous capabilities and opportunities that are opening daily on the World Wide Web.

Somewhere it was said, "I have seen the future and it is weeks away." The concepts and skills it takes to create a useful and attractive Web site are explained in the following chapters in step-by-step fashion from the ground up.

This book makes basic Web page building easy and efficient, starting at the ground floor and working up to more complex topics while avoiding the dynamics of complex programming. The approach is task and event oriented and the full-color graphics make it easy.

In this practical, colorful book, you will learn simple and efficient ways to produce basic, elegant Web pages by utilizing tools that are included on the accompanying CD-ROM. This book will give you a basic starting place to become a proficient Webmaster.

All the software you need to produce great Web sites is included on the accompanying CD as well as the graphics and completed projects from each chapter. If it is not on the CD the URL (Web site address) is given so you can visit and acquire a copy.

After you have installed Internet Explorer and ActiveX Control Pad you will be armed with a basic set of ActiveX controls. You will learn how to add Events and Actions to these controls (with just a point and click!)

and you will be exposed to some basic HTML for scripting purposes. (In the later chapters you will be asked to "plug in" a few lines of code to make certain controls work properly, but nothing so serious that it could be called coding.) Finally you will learn how to create a Web site from scratch, and even how easily it can be put on the Web.

Where you go from here is up to you.

Bob Algie
Rockford, Illinois
E-mail: ralgie@aol.com

CHAPTER 1

How to Prepare Your System for ActiveX

 Microsoft has a great attitude when it comes to exposing newcomers to the act of Web creation. They want you to "Activate the Internet," and they want you to do it with their tools. What better way can you think of than giving away the software for free? You can install the applications directly from the CD in this book to start creating Web pages right away.

The basic group of applications you need to install to create a Web site are the Microsoft® ActiveX™ Control Pad, which gives you a point-and-click environment for creating basic Web pages; Internet Explorer 3.0, the Microsoft Web browser; and the Internet Explorer Multimedia Gallery, which will present you with a variety of specialized graphic themes. Other Web page development tools are available on the Web and commercially, but these three are the only ones you need to get started.

As you go through this chapter, perform all the tasks listed. Your success with creating Web pages during the rest of the book will depend upon the foundation you lay in this chapter.

How to Organize for Web Site Creation

Good file management will save you hours of frustration and development time. Take some time now to set up your system for holding the Web files you'll create.

1 Click on Start in the Windows 95 Task bar. Then choose Programs and click on the Windows Explorer icon to open it.

7 Repeat steps 3 through 5 to create a new folder under CPad1 if you need to.

2 In the left window, select the drive where you want to store your information. Click on the letter of that drive.

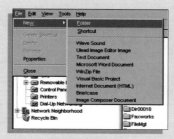

3 Click on the File menu on the Menu bar and choose New. Then click on Folder.

4 At the bottom of the Contents window, an icon will appear with the words New Folder highlighted.

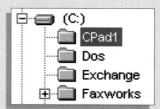

5 Type in the name of your new folder: **CPad1**. Then press Enter. A new folder is created on your hard drive with that name. Look for CPad1 on the CD. You can copy the files you need from that folder.

6 You are going to download graphics also, so you might want a folder below your CPad1. Click on your CPad1 folder in the left window to highlight it.

How to Install Programs from the CD

Load your files directly from the CD. After you install Internet Explorer, ActiveX Control Pad, and the Multimedia Gallery, you can build great pages with very little effort. Follow these few simple guidelines, and you will be ready to go in a jiffy.

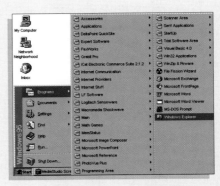

► **1** Open your Windows Explorer by clicking on Start, then choosing Programs. Click on the Windows Explorer icon.

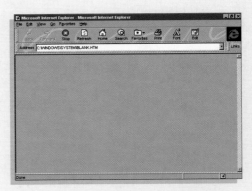

6 To install the Internet Multimedia Gallery, locate the mmgallry folder on the CD. Each theme is a self-extracting file. If you double-click on the theme, you can then just follow the directions for installation.

2 Find your CD drive in your drives box (it's usually drive D) and click on it to view a listing of the contents of the CD.

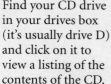

3 Locate the file name of the particular file that you want to install. In this case, look for the Internet Explorer 3.0 file, called MSIE30M.exe. Double click on the name of that file.

Background

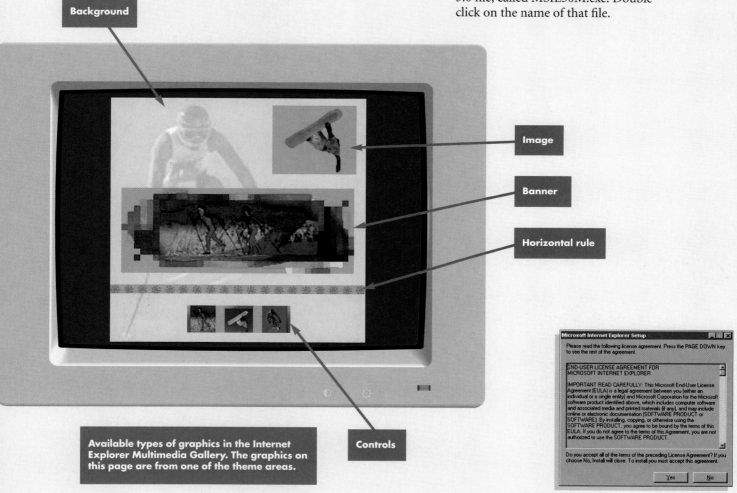

Image

Banner

Horizontal rule

Available types of graphics in the Internet Explorer Multimedia Gallery. The graphics on this page are from one of the theme areas.

Controls

4 You may see the End User License Agreement or an installation wizard. Read and agree to the license agreement, and follow the steps in the wizard.

5 You may see a message box regarding disk space requirements. Click Yes and continue with the setup until it is complete. If you don't have enough disk space, you will have to remove old files or programs to get it.

How to Install the ActiveX Control Pad

The ActiveX Control Pad is a great way for beginners to create versatile and eye-catching Web pages without knowing much about HTML code. Let's go through the simple step-by-step download from the CD to your system.

▶ **1** Locate the folder named Programs on the CD and click on it. Find this folder using Windows Explorer.

6 When the setup is finished, you will receive a message that tells you it was completed successfully. Click OK and the ActiveX Control Pad is ready to use.

2 Locate the file named setuppad.exe (it has an icon of an open box in front of it). Double-click on this self-extracting file, and the installation process will begin.

3 Click "Yes" on the License Agreement, and the file extraction process will automatically begin.

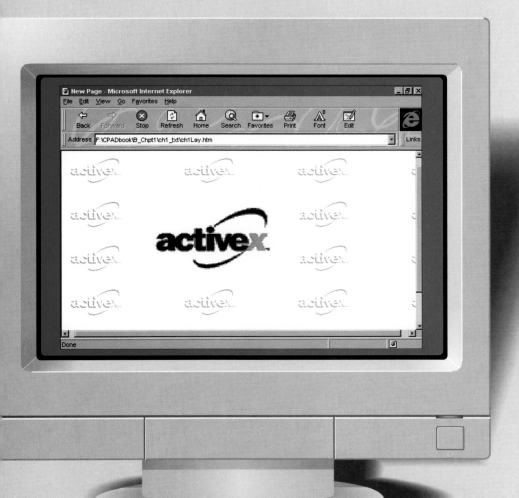

4 When the Microsoft ActiveX Control Pad Setup screen appears, click on "Continue."

5 Follow the directions on your screen to make a complete installation.

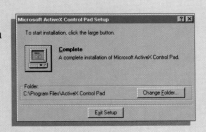

CHAPTER 2

What Are ActiveX and the ActiveX Control Pad?

Each and every ActiveX control adds some sort of function to a Web page. A control can be as simple as a picture or a button you click to go to another location, or it can be complex enough to house many controls with varied functions. Instead of attempting a difficult task with a programming language, you can simply add an ActiveX control to a Web page with a flick of the wrist and a click on your mouse.

The ActiveX Control Pad is a free set of ActiveX controls that you can easily install from the CD (setuppad.exe) or download over the Internet. With this toolbox you can place controls on a page, move them around, duplicate them, control how they work (Events), control what they do (Actions), control what they are (with properties and methods), and a great deal more—as you will soon discover.

The Active part of ActiveX goes with Microsoft's tag line of "Activate the Internet." The "X" seems to be there to mystify us, although Microsoft insists it has some other meaning. Put it all together and you get high performance with simple point-and-click tools.

What Are the Main Features of the ActiveX Control Pad?

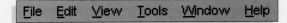

The ActiveX Control Pad gives you a visual, easy-to-use environment for creating Web pages. As you can see in the large graphic on this page, the ActiveX Control Pad main screen offers the Menu bar, the toolbar, and the ActiveX HTML Text Editor. The main part of this screen is the HTML Text Editor, which contains all the necessary tags in its template to enable you to write Web pages painlessly.

1 The Menu bar contains the important elements that are necessary to run the ActiveX Control Pad.

TIP SHEET

▶ **Get familiar with these menus and buttons before you start creating a Web page. They will assist you in producing your Web site.**

▶ **When working with the ActiveX Control Pad along with other applications, do not forget that you don't have to quit this program to go to another. Just click on the little minus (-) box in the upper right corner of your screen to place the program on hold in the Windows 95 Task bar. You can click it back whenever you wish.**

5 The HTML Text Editor is the heart and soul of the ActiveX Control Pad. The Text Editor will become a container for the main files and controls in your Web pages.

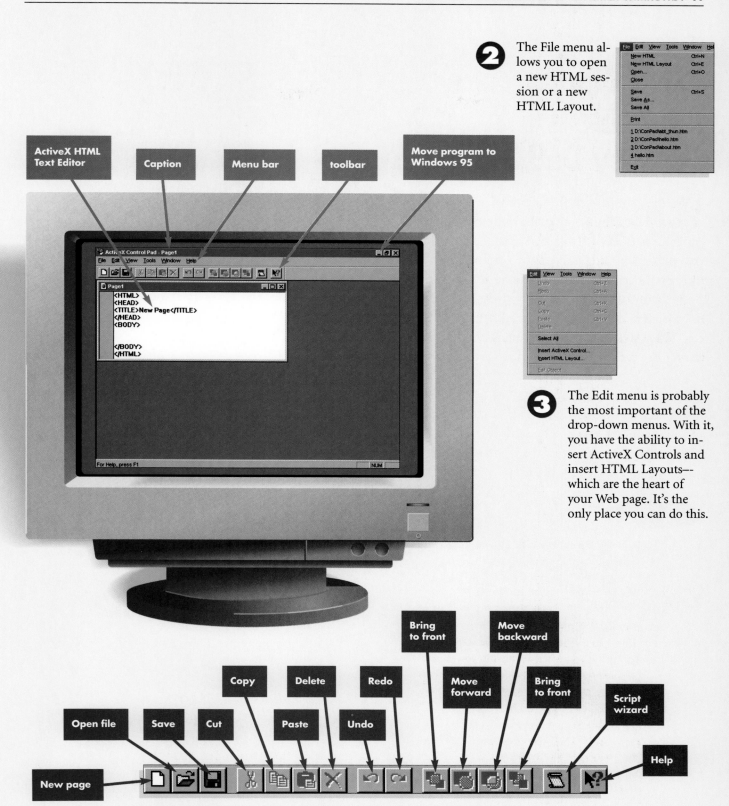

2 The File menu allows you to open a new HTML session or a new HTML Layout.

3 The Edit menu is probably the most important of the drop-down menus. With it, you have the ability to insert ActiveX Controls and insert HTML Layouts—which are the heart of your Web page. It's the only place you can do this.

ActiveX HTML Text Editor

Caption

Menu bar

toolbar

Move program to Windows 95

Bring to front

Move backward

Move forward

Bring to front

Copy

Delete

Redo

Script wizard

Paste

Undo

Open file

Save

Cut

Help

New page

4 Just above the HTML Text Editor and below the Menu bar you will find the ActiveX Control Pad toolbar. This contains buttons for the most frequently used commands from the Menu bar.

What Controls Are Available and What Do They Do?

When you install the ActiveX Control Pad you get a basic set of 14 controls. An ActiveX control is a self-contained object that you place on your Web page to change how the page looks or acts, such as a headline, a picture, or a menu for your readers to click. These basic controls are all you need to create great interactive Web pages. If, after mastering these limited controls, you discover that your Web pages need more specialized functions, you can find other controls on the Internet (or even already installed on your computer!) that suit your more advanced needs. The table at right explains a little more about the controls you get with the ActiveX Control Pad.

TIP SHEET

▶ **The Internet Explorer Web Browser is the first Web browser to support ActiveX controls in Web pages. ActiveX controls can also be viewed in the Netscape Navigator by using the ActiveX Plug-in for Netscape (available at http://www.ncompasslabs.com).**

▶ **Besides the controls you installed with the ActiveX Control Pad from the CD, you might have other controls available on your system. After you've installed the Control Pad, check the control list on your system.**

▶ **Any control you have can be incorporated into your Web pages. Experimentation is the keyword here. Don't be bashful.**

▶ **When selecting a control in the Insert ActiveX Control dialog box, you can speed things up a little by double-clicking on the selected control instead of clicking on the control name and then again on the OK button.**

 To view names of the various controls on your system, click on the Edit option of the File menu and then click on the insert ActiveX Control selection.

When the Insert ActiveX Control dialog box appears, you can page through the control list to see the controls that are available to you with the ActiveX Control Pad. These are listed in the table below.

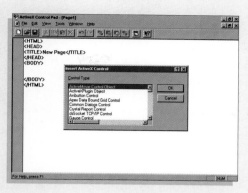

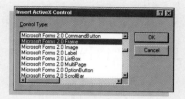

 To add a control to your page, you merely highlight it with a mouse click, then click on OK.

CONTROL NAME	FUNCTION
Microsoft Forms 2.0 Label	Contains basic text labels. Use for titles, headlines, and icons.
Microsoft Forms 2.0 TextBox	Multiline text entry and text display window. Also for data entry.
Microsoft Forms 2.0 ComboBox	Allows your users to choose from a drop-down list of options.
Microsoft Forms 2.0 ListBox	Allows your users to choose from a scrollable list of options to perform various actions that you've specified.
Microsoft Forms 2.0 CheckBox	Allows users to check an option to produce an action or enter data.
Microsoft Forms 2.0 Option Button	Allows users to choose between multiple options for entering data and answering questions.
Microsoft Forms 2.0 Toggle Button	A button that can be toggled on or off.
Microsoft Forms 2.0 Command Button	The basic push-button control. A favorite, and one you use all the time.
Microsoft Forms 2.0 Tabstrip	Provides multiple pages users can choose via tabs. Kind of like a stack of file folders.
Microsoft Forms 2.0 Scrollbar	Basic horizontal and vertical scrollbars. Used when your info is too big to fit in your window.
Microsoft Forms 2.0 Spin Button	A button that can be pushed up or down to display different information or choices.
The Microsoft Image Control	An important control that can display progressively rendered images, for including larger images and backgrounds on your page.
The Microsoft HotSpot Control	A transparent control that can be used to create clickable regions on a page, especially for making buttons that take your readers to other Web locations.
The Microsoft Web Browser Control (Shell Explore control, included with Internet Explorer 3.0)	A control that can display and browse ActiveX documents, including any HTML documents and any other Active Document types (Microsoft Word documents, Microsoft Excel spreadsheets, and so on). This is your viewer.

How to Operate Web Pages

Once created, each Web site must perform certain basic functions. From the opening screen you have to be able to go to a selected page, then to return to your home page. You also have to be able to go to other Web sites by following links (usually shown in highlighted text). To see how this works, use Internet Explorer to open the following site, "Nature Needs Help!," which is on the CD in the file named Nature1.htm in the CPad2 folder.

ActiveX HotSpot controls move the viewer to other pages.

ActiveX HotSpot control moves you directly to the Microsoft Internet Explorer home page.

 1 The opening screen of the "Nature Needs Help" Web site is fairly straightforward. The four pictures on the left (leaf, starfish, spider, and the logo) will take you to other pages in the site. The Internet Explorer logo on the bottom right will take you directly to the IE area at Microsoft. For this demonstration, click on the single brown leaf at the upper left of the page.

TIP SHEET

▶ **These pages were created using only the ActiveX Control Pad, its HTML Text Editor, and its HTML Layout control. You'll learn to use these tools in this book. Of the some 147-plus ActiveX controls in this site, every one was put on the page with just a few clicks of the mouse—*not via* complicated programming!**

▶ **Many of the graphics files here are from the Internet Explorer Multimedia Gallery, also included on the CD. For your Web sites, you can use these graphics, or create your own.**

2 The screen that comes up from clicking on the leaf image gives you the option of going to another page, going back to the home page, or selecting any one of the eight ActiveX CheckBox controls listed on the left. Try clicking on the CheckBox controls first, to see the images change. Next, click on the figure above the words, "Wildlife Preservation."

Before images are activated.

3 The "Saving Our Animal Kingdom" page is similar to the previous page, but it uses different controls to perform the work. Try any of the eight ActiveX CommandButton controls listed on the left by clicking on them. This time, the navigational tools are on the right side of the screen. You've seen the top two already, so click on the spider image to get to the next page.

After images are activated.

4 Using the ActiveX Control Pad, you can create Web sites just like this one. For each element of the page (such as an image or a clickable button), you'll simply choose the control from a list, place it on the page, and tell it what to do. With just a few mouse clicks, you can make an interactive site like this one.

CHAPTER 3

How to Prepare Your System for Web Page Production

 This chapter covers the steps that you should take in preparation for the creation of your first Web page. If you take these few steps, you will be ready. If you don't, you *may* be ready, but there are no guarantees. Once you are fully prepared, you can blaze through your first Web page.

Here again is a list of the software you need for use with this book:

▸ Windows 95

▸ Internet Explorer 3.0, or Netscape 2.0 or greater with the IE Plug-in (available at http://www.ncompasslabs.com)

▸ Microsoft Internet Explorer Multimedia Gallery

▸ Microsoft ActiveX Control Pad

How to Launch Internet Explorer and ActiveX Control Pad

When you build a Web site, it will be necessary to constantly flip back and forth between the ActiveX Control Pad and the Internet Explorer. This constant checking and testing will help you ensure a smooth working Web site in the end. It will also decrease the amount of time you need to spend in experimentation. The following is one good method for achieving this.

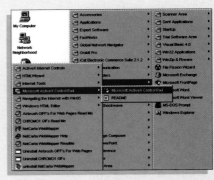

▶ ❶ Open your ActiveX Control Pad by clicking on Start, Programs, and then locating the ActiveX Control Pad and clicking on it.

❾ Once both Internet Explorer and ActiveX Control Pad are launched, it is easy to flip between the two programs—just use the Windows Task bar at the bottom of the page.

❽ Your Windows 95 Task bar at the bottom of the page will now contain the two items—and you are now ready to start on your first Web page. Hooray!

TIP SHEET

▶ **Ignore anything else you might have on the Task bar other than Internet Explorer and ActiveX Control Pad. They are all you need to get started.**

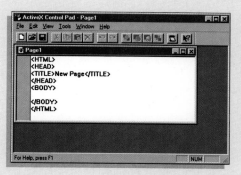

2 Click on the minus (-) box in the upper right corner to move the program to the Windows 95 Task bar.

Microsoft Internet Explorer

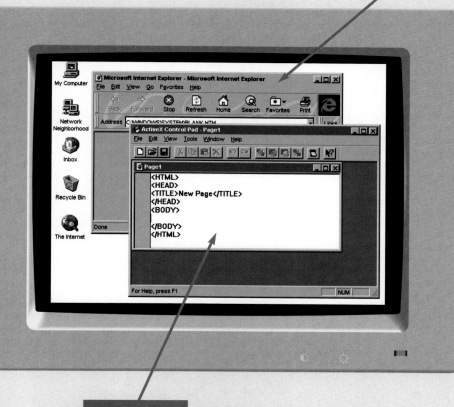

Microsoft ActiveX Control Pad

7 Click on the minus (-) box in the upper-right corner to move the Internet Explorer to the Windows 95 Task bar.

3 If your Internet icon is on your desktop (that's the opening screen when you start Windows 95), all you need to do is double-click on it to start the Internet Explorer.

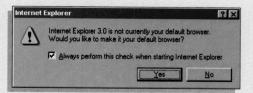

4 If your Internet icon is not on your desktop you will have to open Internet Explorer with the same method you used to open the ActiveX Control Pad. Click on Start, slide up to Programs, and click on the Internet Explorer icon. Although the Internet icon is part of Windows 95, it is also used by Internet Explorer when you install it on your system.

5 If the Internet Explorer is not your default browser (the one that starts when you double-click the Internet icon), you will see this dialog box. Either way you choose, un-check the box marked "Always Perform This Check When Starting Internet Explorer."

6 When the Connect To box comes up, click on Cancel. You don't need to connect to create your Web page, you just need the browser program to test your pages. (If Internet Explorer is your primary browser, you may not see this particular dialog box. If you are connected to a LAN, you won't see this box at all.)

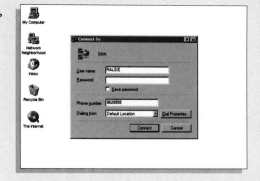

Hardware You Will Need to Create a Web Page

This chapter will serve as a checklist for your system. If you've got the right hardware together, you are ready to go on with this book. If you don't have the proper hardware, perhaps you should take a time-out to get the pieces you need.

▶ **1** You are going to be staring at your monitor a lot. An SVGA or EVGA monitor will serve you best. Your graphics card should be capable of 16-bit or 24-bit color. This is especially true if you will be using photographs in your Web pages. If you are not certain of your graphics capabilities, check the manuals that came with your computer.

TIP SHEET

▶ **If you find yourself in need of equipment upgrades, try some of the mail-order houses that advertise in magazines like *Computer Shopper*. If you can do the installation work yourself, good. If you can't, you may still save a lot of money. If you need assistance with installation, inquire at your local computer retailer.**

▶ **If your computer is a 386, you might be able to upgrade it to a 486 with just a chip. A 486 can go to a 586 or even a Pentium if the number of pins match (check with the manufacturer).**

▶ **A quick solution to the problem of needing more storage is one of the new ZIP drives. Just plug one right in and you are ready to rip.**

▶ **If you are working on a LAN, you don't have to worry about a modem. It's been handled by someone else.**

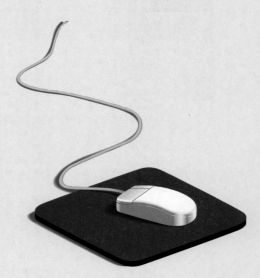

2 It is essential to have a mouse (or other pointing device) that is in good working order. Point-and-click, point-and-click, point-and-click. Voila! A Web site.

2 The Central Processing Unit (CPU) should be a 486sx/33MHz system at the very least, and a Pentium-90 is recommended. Faster is always better and you'll be switching between a lot of screens, so you'll appreciate the speed, so speed will be important to you.

3 You need adequate random access memory, or RAM. The constant swapping of screens and applications during Web site production can use huge amounts of your resources. You could squeak by with 8 Megabytes of RAM, but 16 Megabytes is recommended.

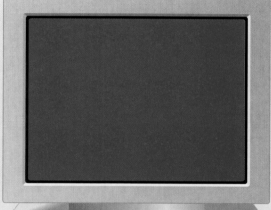

4 You can struggle through with a 14.4 bps rate modem. However, a newer 28.8 unit will undoubtedly make you a happier camper (or a 33.6, or a direct satellite hookup, or a... well, never mind). Any computer less than a year old probably has a 28.8 bps modem or better. Your Internet connection software can tell you how fast your modem is.

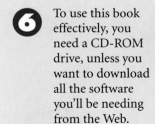

6 To use this book effectively, you need a CD-ROM drive, unless you want to download all the software you'll be needing from the Web.

5 You are going to need lots of storage space on your hard disk while creating a Web site. 50MB of free space should be enough. It all depends upon how extensive your creations are going to become. The final product will only be 1MB to 5MB, because that's all the Internet Service Provider will give you.

CHAPTER 4

How to Plan a Useful Web Site

 Sites on the World Wide Web come to you in absolutely any "flavor" you can imagine. When visiting these Web sites, your emotional state can run the gamut from joy to utter confusion and frustration, depending upon how much Web experience you have. Much of this reaction is due to how carefully planned the site is —or isn't. If everything was thought out and tested in a rational and systematic manner, the chances are that you will enjoy the site and return again. However, if the site is "junk" in the first place, it might as well not even be put on the Web.

It's tempting to start with the images and graphics you have in mind for your site and we will cover that in later chapters. So don't start there! Plan first, embellish later. Always view your Web creation ideas as if you were trying to solve a problem. When all the problems and loopholes are worked out, you will be able to deftly guide your viewing audience to a final destination of your (their?) choosing. Make it a pleasant journey in a hyperdrive space environment, rather than a trek through a rocky and nearly impassable mountain trail.

Before you begin to establish a Web presence, determine your reasons for doing so. Is it to establish name recognition or corporate identity? Is it to provide a service or information? Do you want to sell a product online? Consider also how much time it will take to maintain your site. Once these and whatever other issues that will spring up are cleared up, you can introduce the graphical element to your Web site.

How to Develop a Concept

Research is very important, including analysis of similar features in various sites such as types of buttons, graphics, dividers, and use of type fonts. Early on you should clearly define your objectives and goals. Should your site be friendly, informationally rich, educational, or visually stimulating? You should brainstorm, plan to play with your graphic and verbal elements, and above all, experiment.

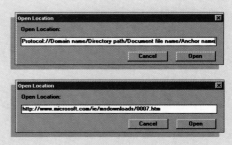

1 Understand a little Web page language (URLs, etc.). The subject will be touched upon at the end of this chapter.

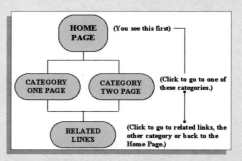

7 Develop a minimal flow chart showing the various levels you need to create. Understand where your viewers are going, where they are, and where they have been at any particular time.

TIP SHEET

▶ When touring Web sites for ideas, keep in mind how annoying some sites can be. Try to identify what it is that you don't like about the site. Does it take too long to download? Is it difficult to navigate? As you become more experienced you will learn how to avoid some of these pitfalls.

▶ If you have any questions or you want to know more about a certain site, the e-mail address of the site creator is almost always listed at the bottom of one of the pages.

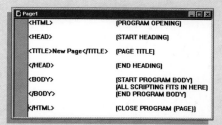

2 Understand just a little bit about Hypertext Markup Language (HTML). You'll get pretty proficient at this the more you get into Web page creation. What you see here is just a sample. There are entire books that explain HTML in great detail, but for a minimal overview on the subject see the last section in this chapter

3 Tour the Web. There is much to be learned about effective Web pages from the amateurs as well as the pros.

4 Consider content. What do you want in your Web site? Is this for personal use, business, or both?

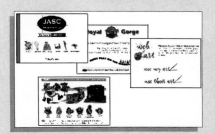

6 Develop a theme. Decide on a "look" and a "feel" for your site.

5 Consider the many variables that your audience will carry to your site, such as age, education level, and "nerd quotient." Consider how elements of your site might affect their experience; what types of text, graphics, and navigation methods will they best respond to? Concentrate on your audience's needs, and make sure your site meets those needs. In particular, be sure to provide a mechanism for your audience to give you feedback about how well your site is doing.

How to Develop a Web Site Road Map

Before you ever get to the graphical element, you should continue your planning with a flow chart or road map of your site. Know where you are going and where you've been at all times. Know how many levels you expect to create and what kind of interactivity you will have between the various levels in your site. Don't use a computer for this. Just grab a piece of paper and get your ideas jotted down.

▶ **1** Level 1 will be your opening, attention-capturing home page. You need a plan for that specific page. Be sure you know what you want that page to do. Most home pages set the tone for the site and contain navigation cues for how to get around in the site.

TIP SHEET

▶ **Design, communicate, and persuade first. Stylize later.**

▶ **Be realistic about the glitz. Keep it fairly simple. The use of too many colors or too many bells and whistles slows down loading time and bothers viewers.**

▶ **If you are not careful, Web sites can become extremely complex, with many levels. Keep asking yourself, What's important? Where am I guiding my viewer? Am I supplying useful information?**

▶ **Continually analyze your information. Understand what actions will take your viewers through your site. Streamline your text by identifying the "key words" of your ideas and setting them off from the rest of the text with boldface, italics, colors, or titles. Remember, people don't usually read, they scan.**

6 Develop your graphics and graphic design after you have a shell (words only) layout that works. Keep it clear and easily understood at all times.

2 The first level is the most important, because this is your chance to grab your viewer's interest. Say something about the company or its services. Use a name or logo. Then direct the viewer's eye toward available interactions, such as going to related topics, other similar pages, or a page in your site that contains the right information.

3 For each level you'll have, list on paper the graphical elements you have available, such as logos, personal pictures, sketches, and other graphics. Gather the corresponding electronic files in one place for creative reference. This can be done for each level and each page in a site.

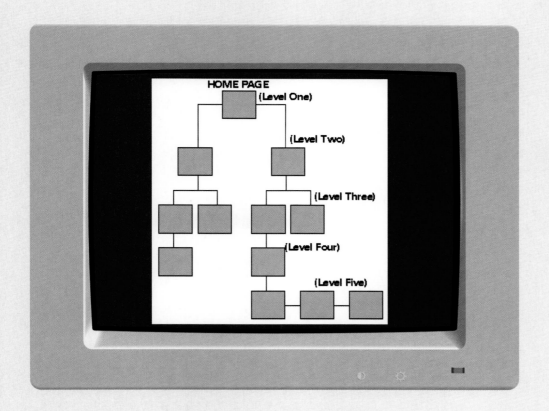

4 As you branch out on Level 2, you will be adding lots of detail. Your viewer (client) is expected to go here looking for something more specific that's related to your home page, as long as your home page was a grabber to begin with.

5 Level 3 is for both resources and the actual information that is being sought. Such things as media galleries and actual downloads are found on this level.

How to Lead Your Viewers around the Web Site

Always put your "hook" on the opening grabber page to set the pace for the remainder of the site. A "hook" is an old advertising term for an attention-getter. It can be as simple as using the same logo on every page.

Be consistent from page to page in your design. Graphics should flow, tell a story, and stimulate your viewer's imagination.

▶ **1** Create initial interest with a good opening page: simple, uncluttered, and informative. Make the viewer wish to press on.

Dangerous Ideas

Kids Stuff

6 When using text, make the characters convey the feeling of the word. With straight HTML coding, you don't have much control in this area. However, the ActiveX Control Pad with its Script Wizard gives you the versatility of a Windows-supported word processor. Whatever fonts and sizes are available in your computer are available on your screen.

TIP SHEET

▸ **Some excellent and very detailed books are currently available on Web site design that you can browse through at your local bookstore. There are also many helpful articles and helpful hints at the Microsoft Web site.**

2 Form a mental image of the physical layout. Always consider the decision making needed to reach the destination of your choice.

3 Increase readability through consistent page design.

4 If you can, create a visual story line for your viewers to follow.

5 Have a "hook" in every section. A "Tip Of The Week," or a link to other neat sites, is appropriate.

How to Hyperlink and Cruise the Web Site

A hyperlink can be an activated section of type, a graphic, or a button that takes you to a specific destination or presents you with some information. When we use the term *hyperlink,* we are speaking of the plan for how the viewer will move around (navigate) the Web site. A good navigational design is determined by how well the site designer links everything together. At this time, we are only concerned with 2-D (two-dimensional) navigation tools, which include text links and inline graphic links. These will get your viewers to the other levels of the site.

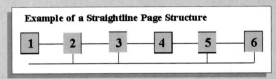

Example of a Straightline Page Structure

1 The simplest navigational structure — and one that is useful in most basic and personal sites — is linear navigation. This is like a simple slide show. Viewers have the option of progressing through the pages, 1, 2, 3, 4, 5, 6 or they can go from any page to any other page, say 6 to 2 or 3 to 5.

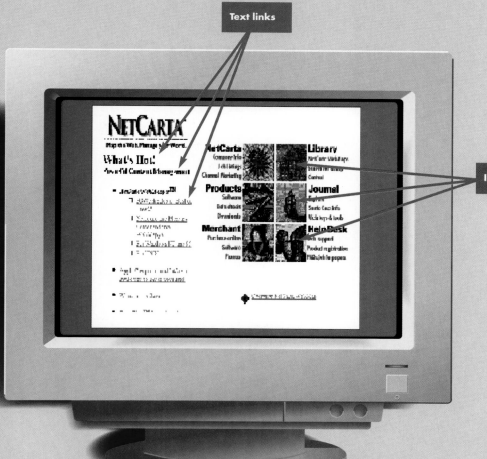

Example of a Hierarchical Page Structure.

2 When Web sites become more complex, the navigational structure must change. Most complex sites use a hierarchical tree.

For more information on the Microsoft ActiveX Control Pad:

- Download the ActiveX Control Pad 1.0. (If you've already installed ActiveX Control Pad, read about the October 4 update.)
- Read the ActiveX Control Pad white paper.
- Step through the ActiveX Control Pad tutorial.
- See authoring tips for the HTML Layout Control.
- Link to sample pages created using the ActiveX Control Pad.
- Review the ActiveX Control Pad FAQ.
- Access the ActiveX Control Pad discussion and user-to-user support newsgroup.

3 When viewing a site, you can recognize active link text (text that indicates a hyperlink to a page that has yet to be visited) because it has a different color than the surrounding black text.

Text links

Inline graphic links

For more information on the Microsoft ActiveX Control Pad:

- Download the ActiveX Control Pad 1.0. (If you've already installed ActiveX Control Pad, read about the October 4 update.)
- Read the ActiveX Control Pad white paper.
- Step through the ActiveX Control Pad tutorial.
- See authoring tips for the HTML Layout Control.
- Link to sample pages created using the ActiveX Control Pad.
- Review the ActiveX Control Pad FAQ.
- Access the ActiveX Control Pad discussion and user-to-user support newsgroup.

4 After the viewer clicks a hypertext link, the color of the link's text changes so the viewers can see that they have already visited this link.

How to Use HTML by Example

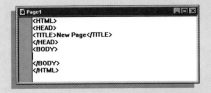

Most of the HTML code for the ActiveX Control Pad and the Microsoft® HTML Layout Control is handled and automatically created by the Script Wizard. However, there are certain times when writing a little simple code can actually be a benefit.

Here is a Web page, with the code that produced each section shown beside it. You don't have to question the HTML code right now, since you'll learn more about it later in this book. This teaser will just show you what HTML looks like.

You can find this code on the CD, in CPad4\HTMLcode.htm. Later in the book, when the need arises, you can edit, cut, paste, and modify this code as necessary.

▶① As we mentioned previously, a lot of the HTML basics are taken care of by the HTML Text editor in the ActiveX Control Pad. The basic template has the opener and closer for the HTML document (<HTML>…</HTML>),the head (<HEAD>…</HEAD>), the title (<TITLE>…</TITLE>), and the body (<BODY>…</BODY>).

TIP SHEET

▸ **You can use any HTML code in conjunction with the ActiveX Control Pad and its HTML Text Editor so the code will perform as you want it to on your pages. Usually, though, you can let the ActiveX Control Pad take care of the coding for you.**

This is the way the URL looks. The first part of the URL is the protocol (machine talk), of which the most common is HTTP, or Hypertext Transfer Protocol. Next comes the domain name of the server you are connecting to. After that comes the directory path of the files you are looking at.

Protocol   Domain name   Directory path

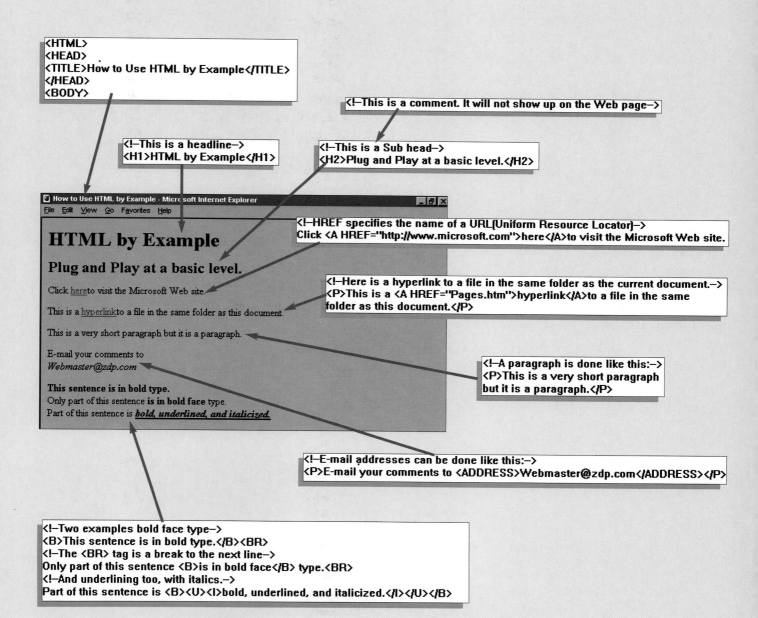

```
<HTML>
<HEAD>
<TITLE>How to Use HTML by Example</TITLE>
</HEAD>
<BODY>
```

```
<!–This is a comment. It will not show up on the Web page–>
```

```
<!–This is a headline–>
<H1>HTML by Example</H1>
```

```
<!–This is a Sub head–>
<H2>Plug and Play at a basic level.</H2>
```

How to Use HTML by Example - Microsoft Internet Explorer

File Edit View Go Favorites Help

HTML by Example

Plug and Play at a basic level.

Click here to visit the Microsoft Web site.

This is a hyperlink to a file in the same folder as this document.

This is a very short paragraph but it is a paragraph.

E-mail your comments to
Webmaster@zdp.com

This sentence is in bold type.
Only part of this sentence **is in bold face** type.
Part of this sentence is ***bold, underlined, and italicized.***

```
<!–HREF specifies the name of a URL(Uniform Resource Locator)–>
Click <A HREF="http://www.microsoft.com">here</A>to visit the Microsoft Web site.
```

```
<!–Here is a hyperlink to a file in the same folder as the current document.–>
<P>This is a <A HREF="Pages.htm">hyperlink</A>to a file in the same
folder as this document.</P>
```

```
<!–A paragraph is done like this:–>
<P>This is a very short paragraph
but it is a paragraph.</P>
```

```
<!–E-mail addresses can be done like this:–>
<P>E-mail your comments to <ADDRESS>Webmaster@zdp.com</ADDRESS></P>
```

```
<!–Two examples bold face type–>
<B>This sentence is in bold type.</B><BR>
<!–The <BR> tag is a break to the next line–>
Only part of this sentence <B>is in bold face</B> type.<BR>
<!–And underlining too, with italics.–>
Part of this sentence is <B><U><I>bold, underlined, and italicized.</I></U></B>
```

CHAPTER 5

How to Create Your First Web Page

 By now you have installed your software, have a good ISP (Internet Service Provider), launched Internet Explorer 3.0, and started the ActiveX Control Pad. Your system is ready and you are anxious to get started.

In this chapter we'll guide you through the initial steps in the creation of your first Web page. You should be able to easily understand how a simple line of code got from the ActiveX Control Pad onto the Internet Explorer screen. When you are done it won't do anything "cool" yet, but you have to start somewhere.

It will be tempting to jump ahead to the later chapters in this book if you already are familiar with HTML. You still need the basics found in these early chapters in order to be able to put the ActiveX Control Pad to work for you.

So let's get started.

How to Use the ActiveX HTML Text Editor

Without the ActiveX Control Pad, you would have to painstakingly lay out your Web pages by hand. But the ActiveX Control Pad lets you do it the easy way. The ActiveX Control Pad contains its own HTML Text Editor and the HTML Layout Control. It is versatile, reliable, and easy to use. It is not only a good place to enter your text, it also has the capability of doing a lot of the "programming" work for you. Press on. ActiveX Control Pad's sorcery will both amaze and delight your creative energies.

TIP SHEET

▶ **Using the ActiveX Control Pad may seem a little repetitive or even slow at times. However, as you proceed throughout the book you will also discover a number of shortcuts to many activities. Persevere! It's worth the trouble to learn the basics instead of learning a whole programming language.**

▶ **View the ActiveX Control Pad as if it was a can of beans. Each bean is an ActiveX control. Put all of the controls together in the right order, apply a little heat (Internet Explorer), and you have dinner (a completed Web page).**

▶ **1** To restore your ActiveX Control Pad from the Task bar, simply click on the Windows 95 Task bar option that holds the ActiveX Control Pad. (You launched it in Chapter 3, so it should already be there. If it isn't, remember to click on Start, select Programs, and open it from your Programs list.)

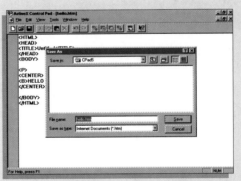

7 In the Save As dialog box type in the new file name **hello.htm**. Don't leave out the .htm part of the file name. Internet Explorer won't recognize the file without it. In the Save In area click on the small window and go to the location you created in Chapter 1 to store your documents. In this case it is the CPad1 folder.

6 After editing the document use the Save As option on the File menu to save the page.

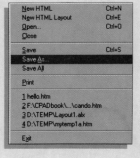

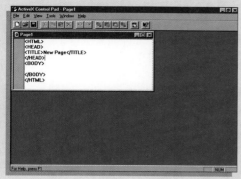

2 The ActiveX Control Pad begins with a blank screen and the small HTML Text Editor in the upper left corner of the screen.

3 You will want to restore the HTML Text Editor to its full size now so you can view and edit the "code" (using the term loosely) you will be working with. This is where all the text and automatically gener-ated code will appear as you are working on your project. The type you see in the editor is a simple HTML template containing the "tags" you will need in the creation of any HTML document.

Menu bar

Toolbar

Maximization & Minimization icon

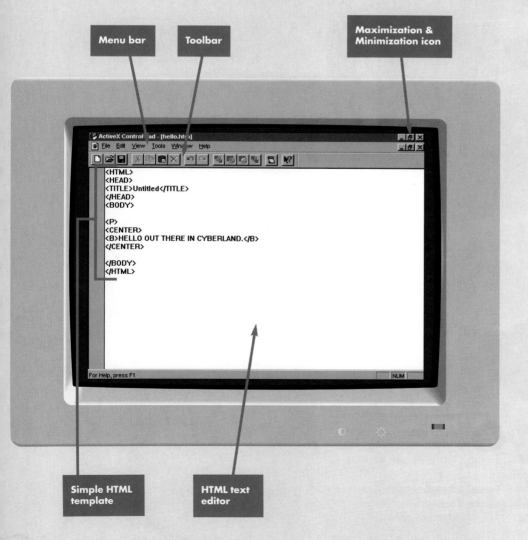

Simple HTML template

HTML text editor

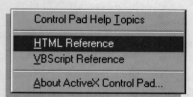

4 When you need more help while using the HTML Text Editor, simply go to the menu bar and click on Help. Then click on HTML Reference.

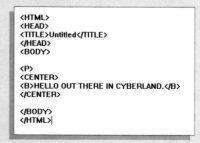

5 Next, you will do your editing (adding the right words in the right places) to the document. Don't worry too much about the HTML code at this point. After editing, your document might look something like this.

How To View Your Page

Much of the magic contained in the production of an ActiveX Control Pad document is controlled by the Web browser working along with various ActiveX controls. You should still have Microsoft Internet Explorer 3.0 minimized (from Chapter 2), so viewing a Web document is only a few clicks away.

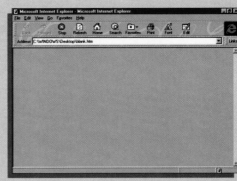

► **1** Drop your ActiveX Control Pad down to the task bar (by using the minus icon) and bring up your Internet Explorer so it fills the screen.

5 When you see the words, **This Web Page Says "Hello out there in Cyberland"** it is ready to be viewed by the world. Look at the original HTML code between the <BODY> and </BODY> tags in the HTML Text Editor of your ActiveX Control Pad.

2 Click the Internet Explorer's Open command on the file menu.

```
New Window    Ctrl+N
Open...        Ctrl+O
Save           Ctrl+S
Save As File...
Send To               ▶
Page Setup...
Print...       Ctrl+P
Create Shortcut
Properties
Close
```

3 Type in the complete path for the hello.htm file in the Open dialog box. (In this case it was **D:\CPad5\hello.htm.**) Click on OK.

```
Open                                      ? X
   Type the Internet address of a document or folder, and
   Internet Explorer will open it for you.
Open:  C:\CPad5\hello.htm                    ▼

       OK        Cancel       Browse...
```

Begin HTML Document

Begin Title

End Head

Begin Body

Paragraph

Begin Center Alignment

Begin Boldface

End Center Alignment

End Body

End HTML document

Begin Headline   **End Title**   **Body Copy**   **End Boldface**

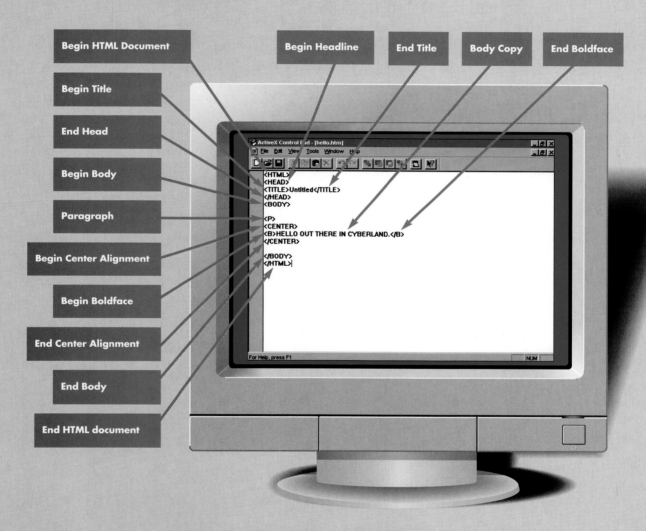

```
ActiveX Control Pad - [hello.htm]
File  Edit  View  Tools  Window  Help

<HTML>
<HEAD>
<TITLE>Untitled</TITLE>
</HEAD>
<BODY>

<P>
<CENTER>
<B>HELLO OUT THERE IN CYBERLAND.</B>
</CENTER>

</BODY>
</HTML>

For Help, press F1                    NUM
```

4 What appears is your first Web page.

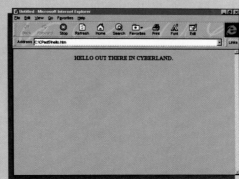

```
Untitled - Microsoft Internet Explorer
File  Edit  View  Go  Favorites  Help

Back Forward Stop Refresh Home Search Favorites Print Font Edit

Address C:\CPad5\hello.htm                        Links

              HELLO OUT THERE IN CYBERLAND.
```

CHAPTER 6

What Are
ActiveX Controls?

 ActiveX Controls are neat little helpers that make your life tolerable as a non-programmer who is creating a Web page. They can add tabs, as on a stack of file folders. They can create interactive buttons to push. They can make words magically appear on your screen or take you to far off destinations on the World Wide Web.

You don't have to write the code that makes these things work, either. Someone else already did that. It's like listening to your stereo. When you want to hear a certain artist all you do is "plug in" a recording, sit back, and relax. In this case the ActiveX Control Pad is your stereo and the ActiveX Controls are like your recordings. And Controls can be almost anything. The ActiveX Control Pad is itself a Control that houses other Controls like the HTML Layout Control.

So plug 'em in, turn 'em on, and off you go in a flurry of interactivity.

How to Add Your First ActiveX Control to Your Web Page

It is time to try out some of the controls that came with your ActiveX Control Pad, discover a little bit about the ways they work for you, and start to experience the ease with which this can be done.

We will start with both our Internet Explorer and the ActiveX Control Pad ready to go and located on the Windows 95 Task bar at the bottom of your screen. With these in place we should be ready to roll.

1 Click on the ActiveX Control Pad on the Windows 95 Task Bar to bring up the Pad on your screen. Maximize your Control Pad and the HTML Text Editor. If you still have hello.htm loaded from the previous chapter, click on File and New for a fresh screen.

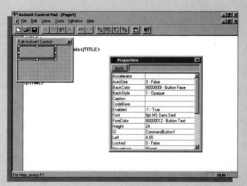

6 When you insert a Control you will then see the Object Editor (smaller window) with the control actually in it, and a Properties Window that houses all the properties of the control. Each object is a container for its properties. The Properties window is used to assign various characteristics, such as a caption, a color, or a picture, to the object.

```
<TITLE>ActiveX Controls</TITLE>
</HEAD>
<BODY>
```

2 In the <TITLE> area of your basic HTML template, replace the words New Page with **ActiveX Controls.**

```
<TITLE>ActiveX Controls</TITLE>
</HEAD>

<BODY>
```

3 Put your cursor just after the <BODY> tag in the HTML Template. This is where you want the ActiveX control to appear.

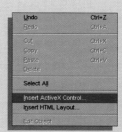

4 Select the Insert ActiveX Control option from the Edit menu at the top of the screen and click on it.

5 The Insert ActiveX Control dialog box will then appear with a list of all the control types available on your system. Choose the Microsoft Forms 2.0 CommandButton control. Command buttons open things, close them, accept results, and so forth. These are the buttons you see on almost every page of almost any program. Highlight the control by clicking on it and then click on the OK.

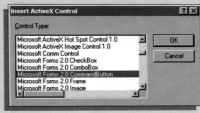

How to Add Your First ActiveX Control to Your Web Page (Continued)

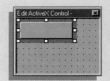 

 7 In the Properties window, double-click on the Caption property and type in **Activate Your Pages Now!** Press Enter. Inside the Object Editor you can resize your control to fit the new caption by holding down your left mouse key and dragging on the white handles. By clicking on the control once you can type words right on the control too.

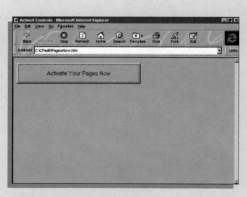

 Take your Control Pad down to the Task bar with the minus (-) icon in the top right corner and bring up your Internet Explorer by clicking on its bar. From the Menu bar choose File and then the Open option to open the PagesNow.htm file to see what you have created. It doesn't look like much yet, but it is a start.

8 To set other properties on this command button you double-click on the property, then perform the necessary action, whatever it may be. To make any property "stick," click on the Apply button in the Properties window.

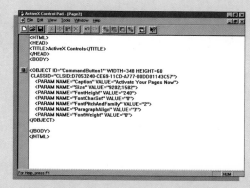

9 If you are finished with the properties, close the Object Editor first (click on the X) and then close the Properties Window to save the creation of the control.

CLICK!

CLICK!

CLICK!

10 Like magic, the <OBJECT> (look for this tag) is created and coded on your HTML page. All of its properties are listed there, as well.

11 Choose the Save As option from the File menu to save your file. Let's name it **PagesNow.htm** and save it in the CPadTemp directory we created in Chapter 1.

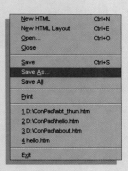

How to Use the Properties Window

When working on a Web page, you will be constantly making adjustments. All sorts of things need to be adjusted, moved, and have their sizes and colors altered before you've got your page exactly the way you want it. The properties window is the place in which you will perform these tasks.

▶ **1** A neat way to track multiple controls on any page is by using the little cube icons you will find next to each control in the left pane of the Text Editor.

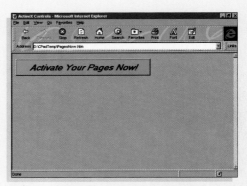

8 Point your mouse arrow to Refresh on the IE toolbar and click. Your newly altered button appears.

7 Reduce your ActiveX Control Pad and bring up your Internet Explorer from the Windows 95 Task bar. The control looks the same. What happened?

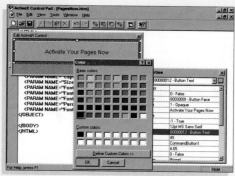

2 To edit an existing ActiveX Control, point to the cube icon and click on it. Your Object Editor and your Properties Window will once again appear.

3 What do you want your CommandButton to do? Let's change the color of the button face. Select BackColor in the Properties Window with your mouse and double-click on it. Select a color, click on it, and then click on OK. Watch the color change on your control.

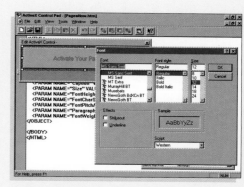

4 In the Font property (double-click on it), let's change the appearance to bold and italic and raise the size to 18 pt. Click on OK again.

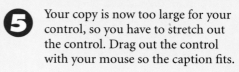

6 Close your Object Editor and then your Properties Window to save your control and its changes. Save the page again from the Save option in the File menu.

5 Your copy is now too large for your control, so you have to stretch out the control. Drag out the control with your mouse so the caption fits.

How to Add a Second Control

The real power of ActiveX is its ability to add multiple controls and then integrate the controls' behaviors by adding scripting. This is how great applications can be built within any Web page. Right now we are just adding controls and setting things up for Chapter 7, where we will make them behave and interact by using the Script Wizard feature of the ActiveX Control Pad.

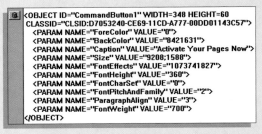

```
<OBJECT ID="CommandButton1" WIDTH=348 HEIGHT=60
CLASSID="CLSID:D7053240-CE69-11CD-A777-00DD01143C57">
    <PARAM NAME="ForeColor" VALUE="0">
    <PARAM NAME="BackColor" VALUE="8421631">
    <PARAM NAME="Caption" VALUE="Activate Your Pages Now">
    <PARAM NAME="Size" VALUE="9208;1588">
    <PARAM NAME="FontEffects" VALUE="1073741827">
    <PARAM NAME="FontHeight" VALUE="360">
    <PARAM NAME="FontCharSet" VALUE="0">
    <PARAM NAME="FontPitchAndFamily" VALUE="2">
    <PARAM NAME="ParagraphAlign" VALUE="3">
    <PARAM NAME="FontWeight" VALUE="700">
</OBJECT>
```

▶ **1** Go back to your Control Pad. If necessary, reopen your file called PagesNow.htm. Position the cursor on the line following the </OBJECT> tag. Insert two line break characters by typing <**BR**> on two consecutive lines.

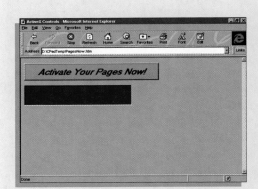

8 Save your control with the File menu, reduce your Control Pad, bring up your Explorer, and click on Refresh on the IE Tool bar. Now two controls appear.

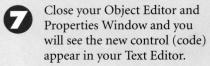

```
<OBJECT ID="TextBox1" WIDTH=303 HEIGHT=59
CLASSID="CLSID:8BD21D10-EC42-11CE-9E0D-00AA006002F3">
    <PARAM NAME="VariousPropertyBits" VALUE="746604571">
    <PARAM NAME="BackColor" VALUE="4210816">
    <PARAM NAME="ForeColor" VALUE="16777215">
    <PARAM NAME="Size" VALUE="7985;1535">
    <PARAM NAME="BorderColor" VALUE="8421631">
    <PARAM NAME="FontName" VALUE="Reindeer SF">
    <PARAM NAME="FontHeight" VALUE="320">
    <PARAM NAME="FontCharSet" VALUE="0">
    <PARAM NAME="FontPitchAndFamily" VALUE="2">
    <PARAM NAME="FontWeight" VALUE="0">
</OBJECT>
```

7 Close your Object Editor and Properties Window and you will see the new control (code) appear in your Text Editor.

2 Insert the second control by selecting the Insert ActiveX Control from the Edit menu.

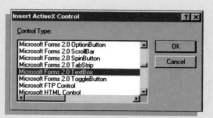

3 In the Insert ActiveX Control dialog box, select the Microsoft Forms 2.0 TextBox Control. This control is mainly for holding text and entering text. Click on OK.

CommandButton Control

TextBox Control

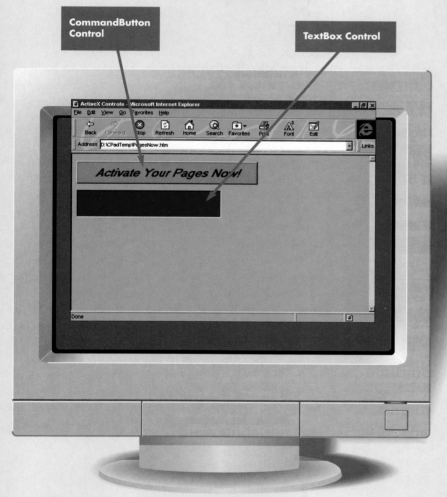

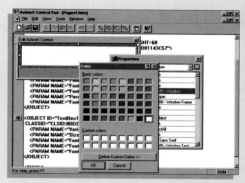

4 The Object Editor will appear with the TextBox in design mode. Don't type in the TextBox. Go to the Properties Window and change the background color to burgundy (any color will do).

6 Black type on burgundy won't show up too well, so double-click on ForeColor. Change it to white by clicking on the small white box, then on OK. In the Object Editor, enlarge your text box to accommodate the new type when it shows up.

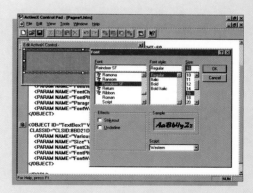

5 In the Properties Window, double-click on Font. Pick an available font you like (this is Reindeer SF) and make it 16 Pt. Then click on OK.

How to Add Other Controls

Before we get into scripting, we should look at several other frequently used controls so you will understand their basic use. When everything is in place, we will move to the chapter concerned with scripting.

1 Repeat steps 1, 2 and 3 from the previous spread (How to Add a Second Control). Now you have to decide which control you want to try out. Select a Microsoft Forms 2.0 Label Control and place it immediately following the </OBJECT> tag. A Label control can hold text, small pictures, icons, and so forth. In the Properties Window, select Caption with a double-click and type in **Stuff I like (Check all that apply)**. Change the Font Property to bold and size to 14. Then click OK. You will notice that the type doesn't fit; you will have to enlarge the Label box with your mouse until it does.

TIP SHEET

▶ **Always keep track of all the ActiveX Controls you are using and make notes on ways to use them again. You might come up with something that nobody else has done before.**

▶ **At this point, you have typed in only 20 or 30 words or short lines. The original HTML Template contained eight lines. Through your careful and diligent mouse maneuverings, you have about 160 lines that the ActiveX Control Pad created just for you.**

▶ **Remember to save your work after each of your modifications. If the Internet Explorer doesn't change when you click on the Refresh button, you probably forgot to save your document first.**

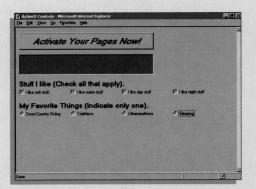

7 To see what you've created, from the File menu select the Save option and save your HTML document. Then reduce your Control Pad, bring up your Internet Explorer, and click on Refresh.

2 Close the Object Editor to insert the new code in the Text Editor.

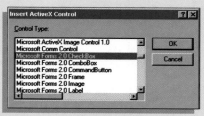

3 Perform the steps necessary to insert a control again. Let's try the CheckBox Control. Select it and click OK. Create three more CheckBox controls to follow the first. These are used for making choices, entering data, opening windows, and so forth. They are usually found in groups.

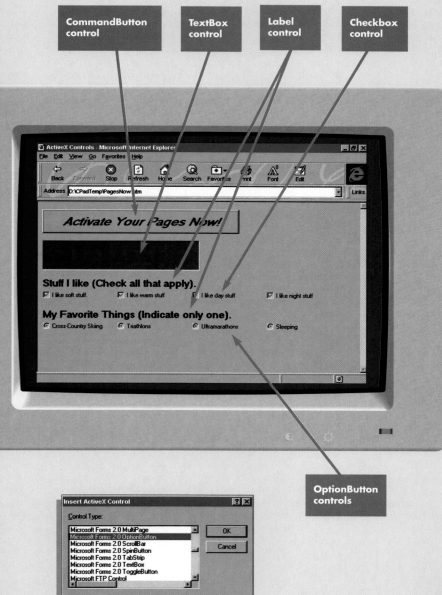

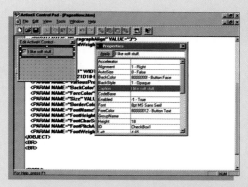

4 In the Properties Window for the first CheckBox, double-click on the Caption property and type in **I like soft stuff.** Close the Object Editor and repeat this for the other three CheckBoxes. Type in the three individual Caption properties to read **I like warm stuff, I like day stuff,** and **I like night stuff.**

5 Insert two **
** (line break) tags after the code for the four CheckBoxes. Now set up another Label Control that reads **My Favorite Things (Indicate only one).** Close the Object Editor to insert the code.

6 Now create a group of four more controls. This time, choose the Microsoft Forms 2.0 OptionButton control. It performs similar tasks to the CheckBox control, but it is round instead of square. In the Caption property of the Properties Window, type in these captions for each of the four buttons: **Cross-Country Skiing, Triathlons, Ultramarathons,** and **Sleeping.**

CHAPTER 7

How to "Program" Script into Your Page

It's time to make your Web page interactive. Up to this point it hasn't been too difficult to create the music to our "Websong." Now we only need some words to make it all come together. That won't be too strenuous either. If you've done everything in this book up to this point you now have an HTML document with 12 embedded ActiveX Controls just sitting there waiting for something to happen. It is time to use the Script Wizard to easily integrate these controls and provide a degree of interactivity.

VBScript, the scripting language built into your ActiveX Control Pad, allows you to capture events from your ActiveX Controls, invoke methods of doing things, modify the properties of the controls, and a lot more.

To better understand what is going on with the Script Wizard you should grasp some of the basic terminology before going ahead. An *event* is something that causes an action to take place. For example, a click event causes a program to start. A *method* is the way an object acts when an event takes place. A *click event* can cause the "clear" method to remove all objects from a collection. An event plus a method results in some action taking place. Lastly, a *property* is a value assigned to a control such as color, size, a picture, or words.

Using the Script Wizard is a wonderful and easy way to coordinate activities in your document, as you will soon find out. In this chapter you will discover some of the ways the Script Wizard empowers your controls. In subsequent chapters you will discover more of the ways the Script Wizard can work for you and your Web pages.

How to Use the Script Wizard

In Chapter 6 you created a lot of controls and placed them on a page. Now you will learn ways to empower those controls to take action. Follow a few quick steps and when you click on a command button words will appear, and when you click on an Option button words will change, as will colors.

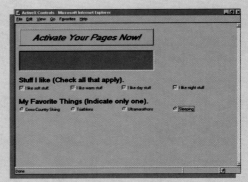

1 Open your "PagesNow.htm" Web Page in the Internet Explorer and in your ActiveX Control Pad.

8 In the Script Wizard's pane #3 (at the bottom) the action that will be taking place will now be shown.

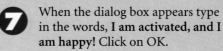

7 When the dialog box appears type in the words, **I am activated, and I am happy!** Click on OK.

 2 On the toolbar, click the Script Wizard icon, or from the Menu bar, choose Tools, then click on Script Wizard.

3 When the Script Wizard materializes this is what you'll see. The upper left (Events) pane shows all the controls you have on your page. The upper right pane is for Actions that an event can cause to happen.

Scripting code for PagesNowButton (automatic)

4 Click on the plus (+) sign next to the CommandButton1 to view all the events that can be attached to this control. The click event is the most common.

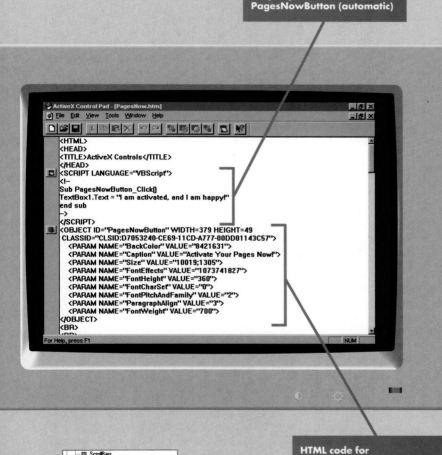

HTML code for PagesNowButton (automatic)

5 In the Event (left) pane click your mouse on the Click event. In the right pane (Actions) select the TextBox1 control and click on it. This will drop down a list of methods and properties. The methods are in yellow and the properties are shown with a blue icon.

 6 Find the Text property in the right pane and double-click on it.

Continue to next page ▶

How to Use the Script Wizard (Continued)

```
<SCRIPT LANGUAGE="VBScript">
<!--
Sub PagesNowButton_Click()
TextBox1.Text = "I am activated, and I am happy!"
end sub
-->
</SCRIPT>
```

▶ **9** Close the Script Wizard by clicking on OK to create more magic. The VBScript code is inserted into your HTML document instantly.

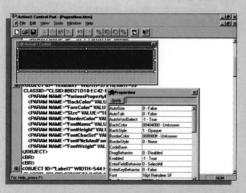

13 Close the Object Editor, click on the Disk icon on the toolbar to save your change, bring up your Internet Explorer and click on Refresh in its toolbar. Now click on your CommandButton (Activate Your Pages Now!) and view the results.

TIP SHEET

▶ Always remember to save your work even with a minimal change. This may prevent surprises.

▶ If for some reason you want to see the code for the control when you are working in the Script Wizard, click on the OptionButton at the bottom of the Window that shows "Code View."

10 Save your PagesNow.htm document by clicking on the Disk icon in the toolbar. This is a shortcut for the Save option.

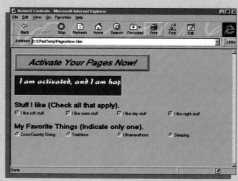

11 Bring up your Internet Explorer from the Windows 95 task bar and click on the IE Refresh button. Then click on your button that reads "Activate Your Pages Now!"

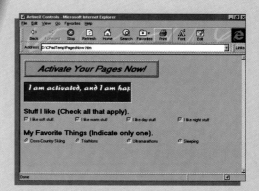

12 Oops! The words didn't fit in your TextBox Control. That's okay. Go back to your Control Pad, click on the little cube icon next to the TextBox code, and physically (with the mouse, of course) stretch the box enough for the words to fit by dragging the edge.

How to Add Actions to Other Controls

Now we should consider our other controls and what we wish them to do. Let's go through the CheckBox Controls first, then you can work with the OptionButton Controls if you want to do that on your own. **CAUTION!** Some of the following steps contain multiple tasks for you to pursue. Take them one "comma" at a time and proceed.

▶ **1** Bring on your Script Wizard in the ActiveX Control Pad by clicking on the Script Wizard icon or by choosing Tools on the Menu bar and the Script Wizard Option.

Mmmm... Feels so good.

8 Click on the check box with the caption that shows "I like soft stuff." The new words will appear in your TextBox Control.

7 Click on the Disk icon in the toolbar to save your additions and changes. Bring up your Internet Explorer and click on the Refresh button to bring in the new version of your Web page.

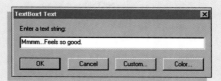

2 In the Events pane select the first CheckBox1 and click on the plus (+) sign in front of it. Then click on the Click Event in that pane.

3 Find the TextBox1 in the Actions pane (right) and double-click on it. Now double-click on the Text property and type in, **Mmmm…Feels so good.** Click on OK.

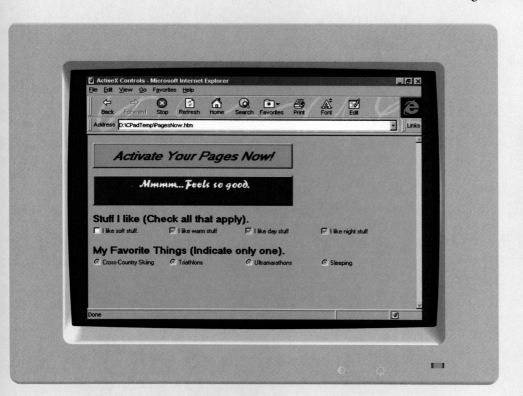

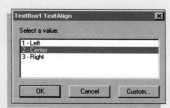

4 Select the TextAlign Action and double-click on it. In the dialog box that appears, select Center by clicking once and then click on OK.

6 The Actions you have created will show up in the lower pane of the Script Wizard. If they appear correct to you click on OK to embed the code in your document.

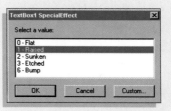

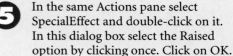

5 In the same Actions pane select SpecialEffect and double-click on it. In this dialog box select the Raised option by clicking once. Click on OK.

TRY IT!

Here is your opportunity to put the knowledge you have gained to work in a step-by-step fashion. Follow these directions and you will create a simple home page, with a couple of twists, that tells a potential customer something about a product and the company that markets it. If you get lost or can't make it work the way you think it should, the files are on the CD to help you.

You will be creating this document from scratch using the HTML Text Editor (and its template) in the ActiveX Control Pad. Be sure to plug in all type exactly as shown so you will get a complete working Web page when you are finished. Later you can go back and use this section as a guide for creating your own home page.

For this exercise you will be using a fictitious company named Thunderbolt, Inc. Its business concerns computer stress management.

1

Bring up (either maximize or launch from the Task bar) the ActiveX Control Pad and maximize the HTML Text Editor that lies inside it

```
<HTML>
<HEAD>
<TITLE>New Page</TITLE>
</HEAD>
<BODY>

</BODY>
</HTML>
```

2

Immediately following the <TITLE> tag, replace the words "New Page" and type in **About Thunderbolt, Inc.** This is the title of the document, which will appear as the window title for this page when it's displayed in a browser. The title does not appear on the page itself.

```
<HEAD>
<TITLE>About Thunderbolt, Inc.</TITLE>
</HEAD>
<BODY>
```

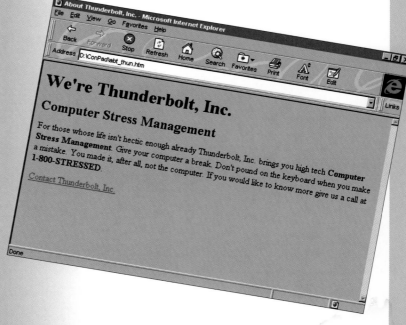

```
<BODY>
<H1>We're Thunderbolt, Inc.</H1>
</BODY>
</HTML>
```

To create a heading for your page type an <H1> tag on the line just below the <BODY> tag. On the same line type **We're Thunderbolt, Inc.** followed by the ending tag </H1>, and press Enter.

```
<BODY>
<H1>We're Thunderbolt, Inc.</H1>
<H2>Computer Stress Management</H2>
</BODY>
```

For a sub-heading, place the cursor just after the </H1> tag and press Enter. On this new line type in **<H2>Computer Stress Management</H2>**. Press Enter to get to a new line. When displayed in a browser, a heading marked H2 will appear a little smaller than the main H1 heading.

```
<BODY>
<H1>We're Thunderbolt, Inc.</H1>
<H2>Computer Stress Management</H2>
<P>
</BODY>
```

To begin the first paragraph, on a new line type <P>. You must use this code each time you start a new paragraph.

```
<BODY>
<H1>We're Thunderbolt, Inc.</H1>
<H2>Computer Stress Management</H2>
<P>For those whose life isn't hectic enough already Thunderbolt, Inc. brings you high tech
Computer Stress Management. Give your computer a break. Don't pound on the keyboard
when you make a mistake. You made it, after all, not the computer. If you would like to know
more give us a call at 1-800-STRESSED.</P>
```

Type the entire first paragraph as shown here. At the end of the paragraph, type </P>, and press Enter. You must always end your paragraphs with this end-of-paragraph marker.

```
<P>For those whose life isn't hectic enough already Thunderbolt, Inc. brings you high tech
<B>Computer Stress Management</B>. Give your computer a break. Don't pound on the
keyboard when you make a mistake. You made it, after all, not the computer. If you would
like to know more give us a call at <B>1-800-STRESSED</B>.</P>
```

Boldface words will stand out in the paragraph better. To make the words "Computer Stress Management" stand out, place the cursor immediately before the words and type <B>. Immediately after the words type the ending tag </B>. Now do the same thing for the phone number.

```
like to know more give us a call at <B>1-800-STRESSED</B>.</P>
<P>Contact Thunderbolt, Inc.</P>
```

Start a new paragraph with another <P>. Then type **Contact Thunderbolt, Inc.** and close the new paragraph by typing </P> on the same line.

```
like to know more give us a call at <B>1-800-STRESSED</B>.</P>
<P><A HREF="contact.htm">Contact Thunderbolt, Inc.</P>
```

You can make this last sentence a hyperlink that points to another document (contact.htm, which we'll create later) that contains the contact information. Position the cursor immediately before the word "Contact" and type **<A HREF="contact.htm">**.

```
<P><A HREF="contact.htm">Contact Thunderbolt, Inc.</A></P>
```

Position the cursor just after the word, "Inc." in the second paragraph, and type the tag </A> to close the hyperlink.

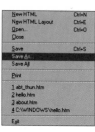

Save the file by first clicking on the File menu and then the line, Save As.

Continue to next page ▶

TRY IT!

Continue below

Type in the File name calling it **abt_thun .htm**. Then click on the Save button. The Web page should be saved to the same folder you used before.

Minimize your ActiveX Control Pad down to the Task bar and bring up your Internet Explorer. Load the new HTML document by clicking on the Open option of the File menu.

In the Open dialog box type in the path for your abt_thun .htm file. For example, if you stored it on your "C" drive you would type -**C:\CPadt1\abt_thun.htm**. Then click OK.

Now you can compare the three distinct screens that show the phases of creating this page. You started with the ActiveX Control Pad and the HTML Text Editor with its HTML template. Next, you created the Thunderbolt Web page by inserting a few well-chosen words and tags. Finally, you viewed the final result on the Internet Explorer. This final page is the one that customers will see on the Web. This simple page looks okay, but a bit boring. So let's add several controls and make something happen.

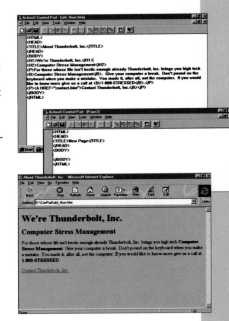

Immediately before the </BODY> tag add a couple of spaces on separate lines by typing in <BR>. The <BR> code is for inserting a line break, without the extra space between lines that you'd get with the <P> tag.

Select the InsertActive XControl option from the Edit menu.

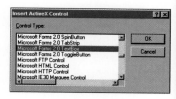

In the Insert ActiveX Control dialog box that pops up select the Microsoft Forms 2.0 TextBox and click on OK.

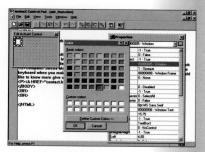

In the Properties Window perform the following operations. Change the AutoSize property to 1 (true) by double-clicking on it. Double-click on BackColor and change it to dark green by clicking once on that color, then once on OK. Change the BorderStyle to 1-Single in a similar way. Change the font to 18-point Shock (if you have it, or something else if you don't have that font). Use double-clicks to change the ForeColor to white, SpecialEffect to 1-Raised, and TextAlign to 2-Center.

Close the Object Editor by clicking on the "X." It's **very** important to close it first. If you close the Properties window first and then the Object Editor, it may not save the code to your Control Pad Window.

```
</OBJECT>
<BR>
<BR>

</HTML>
```

Insert two more <BR> spaces under the TextBox </OBJECT> tag.

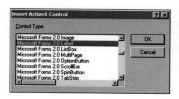

Once again select the InsertActiveXControl option from the Edit menu. In the dialog box select Microsoft Forms 2.0 Label and click on OK.

Follow this step carefully. Here is your double-clicking scenario for this Properties Window: Double-click on the Caption property and type in the Caption, **"Choose the stressful situation you wish to eliminate,"** then press Enter. Double-click the Font property and select Shock (if available) at 16 points. In the Object Editor stretch out the box so the type will fit. Close the Object Editor now.

Below the Label </OBJECT> tag enter one <BR> space. Create an OptionButton Control by selecting the InsertActiveXControl option from the Edit menu, selecting the Microsoft Forms 2.0 OptionButton, and clicking on OK.

Continue to next page ▶

 Continue below

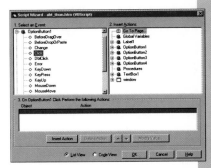

27

Click on the Script Wizard icon on the tool-bar. Select Option-Button1 in the Events pane, click on the plus (+) sign, and click on the Click event.

25

Alter the properties in the Properties Window like this: For the Caption property enter, **"Computer Related Stress."** Make the AutoSize property, 1-True. Change the Font property to match your Label text and make it 12-point. Close the Object Editor to go back to the Control Pad.

28

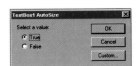

In the Actions pane select TextBox1 and click on the plus (+) sign. Double-click on AutoSize and then OK for "True."

26

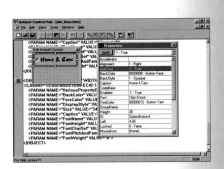

Repeat steps 24 and 25 three more times, to add three more buttons. For these new buttons, your ID property will automatically change to OptionButton **2, 3,** and **4,** and when you enter your Captions, make them **"Business Travel," "Financial,"** and **"Home & Cars."**

29

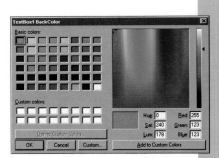

Double-click on BackColor and select a nice warm orange. Click on OK.

30

Double-click on Text and enter the same text as each OptionButton. **"Computer Related Stress," "Business Travel," "Financial,"** and **"Home & Cars."** For each OptionButton click on OK. For TextAlign, double-click and then set it to 2-Center. Click on OK.

31

When all the above is complete click on OK to insert the code into your HTML document.

32

Repeat steps 27 through 31 for Option-Button 2, 3, and 4, inserting the proper text for each button in step 30.

33

Save your work by either clicking on the disk icon in the toolbar or by selecting the Save option from the File menu.

34

Bring your Internet Explorer up from the Windows 95 Task bar and click on Refresh on the Internet Explorer Tool bar.

35

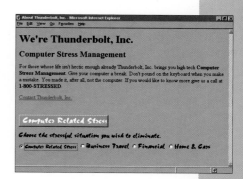

You can see the results of your efforts. Whichever Option-Button you click with your mouse, its text will be displayed in the orange TextBox.

36

Congratulations! You've created a Web page complete with controls that interact with the viewer and with each other.

CHAPTER 8

How to Use the Amazing HTML Layout Control

 So far the on-screen version of the document we have been creating is a single-column, scrolling window that allows changes to its TextBox Control. The next item we'll explore is the Microsoft® HTML Layout Control, which allows us to be more specific about exactly how our page will look, in a design environment that meshes with the ActiveX Control Pad's editing environment.

What does this combination allow? Here's a sampling:

▸ Exact 2-D placement: This means you are given the ability to place other controls anywhere on the page that you want. You can move them around, align them, stagger them, and make them fit exactly where you want them.

▸ Overlapping regions: You can specify the exact order of each control on the page.

▸ Transparency: This is a way users can see through text or objects to images underneath.

▸ Scripting: The HTML Layout Control fully supports scripting, so that any object in a 2-D region can script (enable or disable) any other object in that region.

CAUTION: Many of the steps that follow contain multiple instructions. Perform these steps carefully and in consecutive order for the best results.

How to Insert a 2-D Region into Your Document

With the HTML Layout Control, you don't need to know HTML syntax backward and forward and you don't even need to know all the appropriate tags. Without the ActiveX Control Pad you'd have to do it the hard way, but now you can skip over the "language learning" part and follow these steps to design your pages.

This section shows you how to create 2-D regions, which must be defined as a separate file with an .ALX extension after the file name.

▶ **1** Maximize your Internet Explorer but do not connect to the Internet. You will be using it for editing purposes only.

```
<OBJECT CLASSID="CLSID:812AE312-8B8E-11CF-93C8-00AA00C08FDF"
ID="PN1_alx" STYLE="LEFT:0;TOP:0">
<PARAM NAME="ALXPATH" REF VALUE="PN1.alx">
</OBJECT>
```

7 The special .alx object will be automatically created in your HTML document. This is where the Layout will be saved.

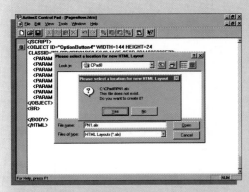

6 From the Edit Menu bar, choose Insert HTML Layout. A dialog box will appear, asking you where you want to store the HTML Layouts (.alx files) you create. Store them in the CPad8 folder with your PagesNow.htm file. Then type in PN1.alx for the file name, then click on Open. Click on Yes when asked if you want to create the file.

2 If you want a a full view of your page, you can hide the toolbar by selecting the View menu and clicking off toolbar. Don't worry, you can get it back anytime by using the same menu that you used to turn it off.

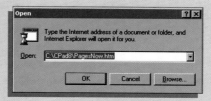

3 Click File, Open, and type in the path for your PagesNow.htm file, such as C:\CPad8\PagesNow.htm. Click on OK.

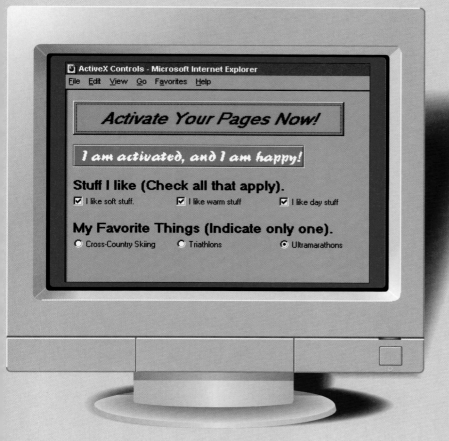

4 Open your ActiveX Control Pad and get your PagesNow.htm file. It is either on your CD in the CPad8 folder or in the CPad8 folder you loaded on your hard drive. Scroll down to the region at the very bottom of the code where we will be adding our HTML Layout Control.

5 Since you will be inserting your HTML Layout Control after the existing controls on the page, locate the region after the last </OBJECT> tag and before the </BODY> tag. On a separate line put in a space <BR> and place the cursor on the line following.

How to Use the HTML Layout Control Toolbox

I n the toolbox you'll find all the available standard components from the ActiveX Control Pad. The big difference is that you don't have to select the ActiveX controls by name. In this case you will select them by clicking on their icons.

To open an editing session on your .alx (HTML Layout Control) file, click once on the .ALX icon to the left of the object.

Many neat things happen here, but the main items to notice are the HTML Layout grid and the presence of the HTML Layout toolbox.

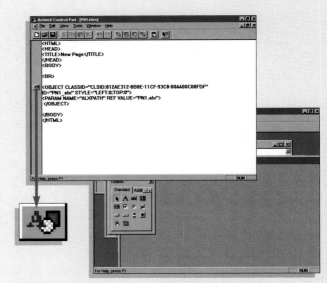

▶ **1** Maximize your grid window to fill the page by clicking on the max/min icon in the upper right corner of the window.

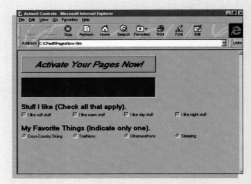

7 Bring up your Internet Explorer from the Windows 95 task bar. Click on View on the Menu bar and then Refresh to view the changes you have made.

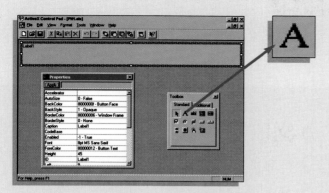

2 Select the Label icon and click on it once. Move the cursor anywhere you want on the page (top left for example) and drag out a Label box. You can alter the size with the handles any time you like. Place the cursor anywhere within the confines of the Label box and double-click to bring out the Properties Window.

3 This Properties Window works exactly the same as it did in the Control Pad. Double-click on the Caption property and type in, **This is the kind of action I like!** Press Enter. Change the Font property to MS Sans Serif, Bold Italic, and 18-pt. Click OK. Double-click on AutoSize and change it to 1-True. Close the Properties Window.

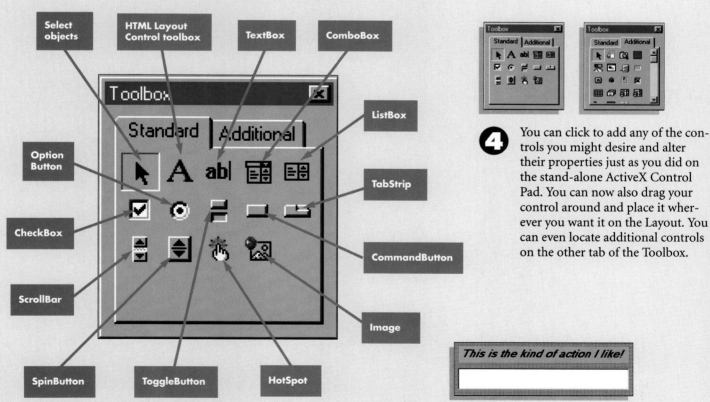

4 You can click to add any of the controls you might desire and alter their properties just as you did on the stand-alone ActiveX Control Pad. You can now also drag your control around and place it wherever you want it on the Layout. You can even locate additional controls on the other tab of the Toolbox.

This is the kind of action I like!

5 For this example, place a TextBox directly under the Label box. Double-click on the TextBox icon, drag it below your Label and resize it by dragging the handles (little squares) to a size similar to the Label.

6 Click on the disk icon in the main toolbar to save the ALX file in its current directory, then click on the .ALX icon in the Menu bar to close the file.

How to Create Duplicate Controls (and More)

You have already created identical CheckBox and OptionButton Controls with just the ActiveX Control Pad. They were all in a straight line and you had no control over placement. It would take a lot of time and HTML code to stack these controls. The HTML Layout Control makes this task child's play.

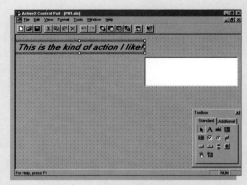

▶ **1** Bring up your ActiveX Control Pad and click on the .ALX icon to edit and use your Layout again. Let's change our TextBox Control and move it over to the right.

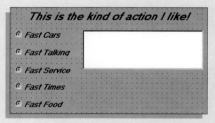

6 Double-click on the Caption property for OptionButton1, type in Fast Cars, and press Enter. Change the Font property to Bold Italic and 12-point. Do the same for the other four OptionButtons but change the Captions to Fast Talking, Fast Service, Fast Times, and Fast Food respectively.

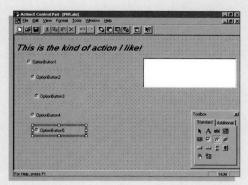

2 Find the OptionButton icon in the HTML toolbox and double-click on it once. Move the cursor to an area on the left side of the layout and click one time. Move below it and click a second time. Repeat this until you have five OptionButtons. To stop placing these controls, point to a blank area in the toolbox and click once.

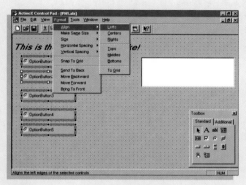

3 You can manually arrange these five OptionButton Controls or you can align them automatically. Drag a box (it will appear as a dotted line) around your five OptionButton Controls. Then click on Format in the Menu bar, slide to Align, and click once on Left.

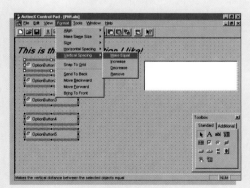

4 The vertical spacing is probably off too, so go back and drag a box around the controls again. Go to Format (click), Vertical Spacing (that's the spacing between the controls), and Make Equal (click). Use the same commands to increase or decrease the amount of spacing between them.

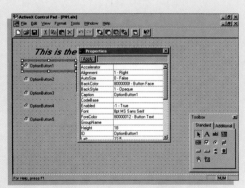

5 To change the properties of your controls, just point at the control you wish to alter and double-click on it. The control will be highlighted and the Properties Window will appear.

Continue to next page ▶

How to Create Duplicate Controls (and More) (Continued)

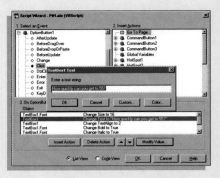

▶ **When aligning controls, note that each command on the menu has a small picture that shows how the controls can be aligned.**

▶ **Do not confuse aligning controls with the TextAlign property. This is for the text located in a ComboBox, Label, and TextBox.**

▶ **The only image file formats that you can use with the ActiveX Control Pad and its HTML Layout control carry the file extensions of .jpg, .gif, .bmp, and .wmf. Other file formats will not work.**

▶ **When laying a HotSpot over an Image control you may experience a slight inconvenience in trying to modify the underlying Image control if it is the same size. Make the HotSpot a little smaller or drag it off the Image, perform your modifications, and then replace it.**

▶ **Another way of duplicating controls is a simple cut-and-paste operation. Do this by clicking on the control you wish to duplicate and then by using the Edit option on the Menu bar (just like a word processor).**

▶ **7** Let's add some script to our controls, starting with Fast Cars. Click on the Script Wizard icon (or Tools, Script Wizard on the Menu bar). In the Events pane (left) click on the plus (+) next to OptionButton1, and then click on the Click Event. Move over to the Actions pane on the right and click on the plus (+) next to TextBox1. Double-click on the Text Action and type in, **How quickly can you get to 55?** Click OK. Double-click on TextAlign and change it to 2-Center (OK). Finally, click on the plus (+) next to the Font and make it Bold (double-click, OK) and Italic (double-click, OK). Click OK to close the Script Wizard.

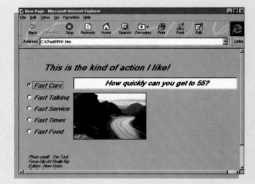

13 Save the Layout by clicking on the disk icon in the main toolbar. Click the .ALX icon and the Close option to close the Layout Control. Save the HTML document with the disk icon again. Now, bring up your Internet Explorer and click on the Refresh option in the View menu.

8 Do the same for the other four OptionButton Controls but make the Text Action read, Now, this might get you in trouble. (for Fast Talking); Something we all seek to give and receive. (Fast Service); Just where is Ridgemont High? (Fast Times); and, Have you checked your Sodium content lately? (Fast Food).

9 To bring in an image, click on the Image icon in the Layout Control toolbox. Drag the picture to the location of choice and drag the frame to the approximate size you want. Let's put it below our TextBox Control. The graphics files you need for this are in the CPad8 folder on the CD or your hard drive if you copied the folder.

10 Click on the HotSpot Control in the Toolbox and drag it to the Image frame you have already created. Drag out the HotSpot but don't fill the Image control area completely or you won't be able to easily modify your Image control. Both the Image and the HotSpot will be invisible at this time.

11 To get the image, double-click on the Image area to call up its Properties Window. To select a picture or graphic double-click on PicturePath and enter the path where the graphic is located (C:\CPad8\roadcurv.bmp). Close the Properties Window.

12 For the HotSpot Control, click on the Script Wizard icon, the plus (+) next to HotSpot1 in the Event pane, and click on Click for the Event. On the Actions (right) side click on the plus (+) next to TextBox1. Double-click on Text and type in, **Really! Are you sure this is fast?** Click OK. Double-click on TextAlign and make it 2-Center. Click the plus (+) next to Font and enable Bold and Italic with double-clicks and clicks. Close the Script wizard by clicking on OK.

How to Modify Actions in the Script Wizard

It seems like nothing is ever perfect. Something is in the wrong place or the type is too small, or the font isn't what you want. You don't have to start over. This is why we have modification and editing capabilities built into our Control Pad.

▶ **1** Bring up your ActiveX Control Pad and open your .alx file by clicking on the .ALX icon.

TIP SHEET

▶ **About clicks and double-clicks: If a single click on something doesn't work, try a double-click. A double-click can sometimes produce an alternative action to occur also. You have to experiment, but remember to keep your index finger limber.**

▶ **Once you are working in the Script Wizard window you can speed things up a little by staying there to modify various controls. Using the Events pane (#1) you can select and click the event and then make the modifications in the code list (#3) at the bottom of the window. Do this for each control you wish to modify, then click OK to exit and save all the modifications at one time.**

7 Save your layout again by clicking on the disk icon. Close the Layout and save the Control Pad document with the disk icon also. Bring up your Internet Explorer and click on View and Refresh in the Menu bar. Try out everything out make any other modifications you might need at this time.

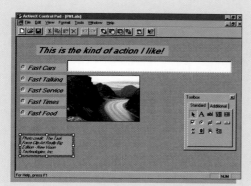

2 Maximize your working area and move the toolbox out of the way by dragging it with your mouse.

3 We're going to increase the type size in the Actions area of the five OptionButtons. Click on Fast Cars and then on the ScriptWizard icon. Click on the plus (+) next to OptionButton1 in the Events pane (top left) of the ScriptWizard. Click on the Click event so the Actions show up below.

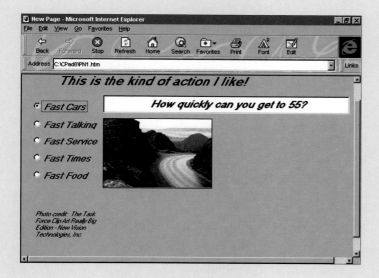

4 In the bottom pane highlight the line that reads TextBox1 Font and click on the Modify Value button.

5 When the dialog box shows up, change the Font size from 12 to 16 by typing in 16. Click on OK. Click the Script Wizard OK to close the screen.

6 Perform the same modification to the other four OptionButton Controls and the HotSpot Control.

How to Enhance Dull Controls

S o far in this chapter you have selected multiple controls, duplicated controls, modified Actions, created an .ALX file, made physical adjustments, and embedded the layout (.alx file) into your HTML document. You didn't do any coding or programming, did you? Some of the controls look pretty plain and visual enhancements are in order. To demonstrate the versatility of the HTML Layout Control, we will now add some further graphic enhancements to your Layout.

TIP SHEET

▶ **For your convenience, all the files used in this spread are located on the CD in the Cpad8 folder. Anything associated with the HTML document (.htm file) that is in use should be available in the same folder. For best results copy the CPad8 folder onto your hard drive before you start performing the steps.**

▶ **Test, test, and test again. One of the keys to a really effective Web page or Web site is the continual testing that you should be doing during each creative step of the way. The more you test your work the better the chance of solving any potential problems that may later arise.**

▶ **If you had to create the code for the illustrations in this spread it might take days. With the HTML Layout Control the time and effort involved has been reduced to a minimum. You are going to create controls here that change type and images. This is the basis for making changes to different pages and different Web sites. Open an .alx file in WordPad and see how much would go into it.**

▶ **1** Bring up your ActiveX Control Pad and open your HTML Layout for editing by clicking on the .ALX icon to the left of the .alx Object code. Maximize your layout to fill the screen.

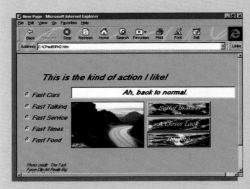

13 Bring up your Internet Explorer. Open the PN2.htm file and try it out.

12 Save the Layout as PN2.alx in the CPad8 folder, close the HTML Layout Control by clicking on the .ALX icon and then on Close. Save the HTML document as PN2.htm.

11 Repeat steps 7, 8, 9, and 10 for Command Button2 and 3. The Caption for #2 is A Closer Look and the Picture property selection is marbb.bmp. The Caption for #3 is Restore, and the Picture property selection is marbc.bmp.

10 The PicturePosition property has a list that drops down when you click on the little "down" arrow. Select 12-Center. This will make your type visible. Resize your Command Button by dragging the handles inward.

2 Go to the toolbox and double-click on the CommandButton icon (a little gray rectangle). Drag-and-drop three CommandButtons next to the image. Move your cursor to a blank area of the toolbox and click once to stop the control duplicating function.

3 Highlight the first CommandButton by clicking on it and open the Script Wizard by clicking on its icon. In the Events pane click on the plus (+) next to CommandButton1 and then click on the Click Event.

4 Move right to the Actions pane. Click on the TextBox plus (+) sign, then double-click on Text and enter. Better than brakes at high speed. Click OK. Change TextAlign to 2-Center, OK. Change Font (+), Bold (True), Italic(True), Size 16.

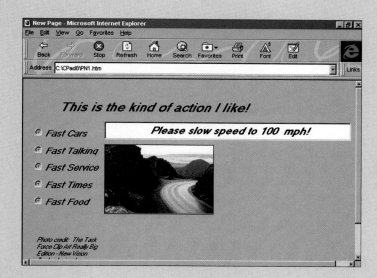

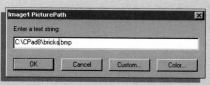

5 Still in the Actions pane click on the plus(+) next to the Image1 Control. Double-click on PicturePath and enter the pathname for your graphic, such as C:\CPad8\bricks2.bmp. Click OK. Also enable the AutoSize Action to True.

6 Repeat steps 3, 4, and 5 for CommandButton2 and 3, substituting the Text in #2 to read, Let's take a closer look, and #3 to read, Ah, back to normal. The PicturePath for #2 is, C:\CPad8\engfrt.bmp, and for #3 it is, C:\CPad8\roadcurv.bmp. Click OK to exit the Script Wizard.

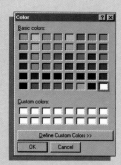

9 Double-click on the Picture property. When the dialog box pops up locate marba.bmp and highlight it with a click. Click on Open.

8 Double-click on ForeColor (Button Text). Select White by clicking on it once and then on OK.

7 Double-click on the top CommandButton to expose its Properties Window. Double-click on AutoSize to change it to 1-True. Double-click on the caption property and type in, **Better Brakes?** Press Enter. Double-click on Font and change it to 12-pt. Bold Italic.

How to Hypertext with the HotSpot Control

Earlier we demonstrated how to use the HTML <A HREF... to hypertext to another page or URL. An example of a hypertext line for contacting a company would be <A HREF="http://www.compuserve.com/workshop">Contact us for more information.</A>, and the words Contact us for more information" would appear in a color different than the rest of the text. With the combination of the HotSpot control and the Script Wizard you will now be given a way to click on any object, area, or control to hypertext your way to other sites. Here's how you do it.

▶ **1** Bring up the ActiveX Control Pad with a new HTML on it. Change the title to Hypertext HotSpot Highway and open a new HTML Layout control in the Body area of the program (Edit, Insert HTML Layout). Name the file HHH.alx.

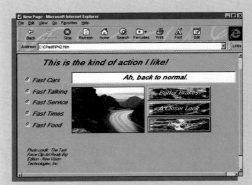

9 As you move the mouse pointer over the image you will notice it changes from an arrow to across. This is telling you the photo has an "active" area. Click on the photo. You have just hypertexted to PN2.htm.

8 Save the Layout and close it. Save the Hypertext HotSpot Highway as HHH.htm in the CPad8 folder. Open the HHH.htm file in Internet Explorer.

2 Open the new .alx object by clicking on it's icon in the left margin. Place a Command-Button control on the left side of the working area as shown here. In the Properties window delete the Caption and change the Enabled property to False. This gives you a small area to work in with your transparent Image and HotSpot controls.

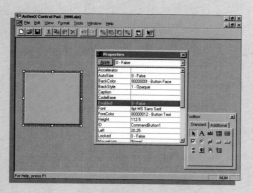

3 Place an Image control inside your new working area and so you can see where it is change the Border-Style property to 1-Single. Set the PicturePath to C:\CPad8\roadcurv.bmp.

4 Place a Label control below the Image and change the Caption property to Click on the photo to go to another site. Change the Font to Bold, Size 10, and TextAlign to 2-Center.

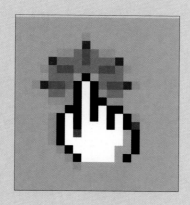

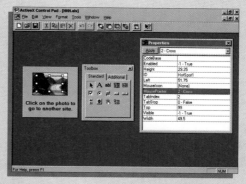

5 Because the Image control does not work alone with a Click Event (like a CommandButton), it's time for our HotSpot control. Place one inside the Image making certain to leave some open area around it's edges. This is so you can still click on the Image to modify it without moving (and perhaps losing) the invisible HotSpot. Change the HotSpot's MousePointer property to 2-Cross.

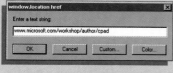

7 If you wanted to go to another Web site from here all you would need to do is enter the words that come after the http:// as shown in the accompanying example. Right now we just want to take you to the page you finished in the last section (PN2.htm). You would need to put a similar control there that was referenced to this site to come back. Click OK to close the Script Wizard.

6 Click on the Script Wizard icon and select the HotSpot1 Event in pane #1 (left). Click on the plus (+) and choose the Click Event. In the #2 pane (Actions) go to the bottom and click on the plus (+) next to "window". Next click on the plus (+) next to "location," and finally double-click on "href."

CHAPTER 9

Frames and Their Use

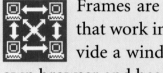 Frames are a way of dividing your Web page into portions that work independently. In the simplest of cases you can divide a window into columns or rows. Each frame acts as its own browser and has the ability to view Web sites independently. This ability to act independently allows you to have several different sets of information on the screen at the same time. You can scroll up and down or side to side in one frame without changing or interrupting the information in the other frames.

Unlike the HTML Layout Control which lets you position ActiveX controls wherever you wish, with frames you can only position controls with the use of HTML code. Of course, you can put HTML Layout controls inside each frame allowing you the same frame independence.

To set up these frames, you describe each one in a separate HTML file, contained by a master HTML file with the overall description of how the page fits together. This is called a frameset. If you have a page with three frames showing, four distinct HTML files are needed: one for each of the frames and one that describes how the frameset will be laid out. These are the basic necessities of frame-based pages.

The best way to gain an understanding of frames is to create some simple examples and that is exactly what we are going to do in this chapter.

How to Use Frames: Creating Columns and Rows

Before you begin, a little planning is needed. Decide how many rows or columns you want to have on your page. If you did your page layout and design work properly you already should know. Then, using the skills you've gained in previous chapters, create the individual pages that make up those columns. In this example, we'll use doc1.htm, doc2.htm, and doc3.htm from the CD. So copy those files into your CPad9 folder, and let's get started using frames.

TIP SHEET

▶ Bear in mind that empty frames will not show up on a Web page. You need to have at least a few words in the body of the document in order to see the frame borders.

▶ The relative sizes of rows or columns is open to your experimentation. In our <FRAMESET COLS="20%, *, *"> tag the "20%" for column 1 means it will take up the first 20% of the page width. The following "*, *" means the remaining area will be divided equally.

▶ From a frame you can point and click to any other Web site. With HTML code you can use the <A HREF="...">...</A> tag set. If you are using ActiveX controls it can be accomplished with the Script Wizard.

▶ Unless the <NORESIZE> attribute is attached to the frame tag, frames can be resized.

1 Open the Microsoft ActiveX Control Pad and maximize it and the HTML Text Editor.

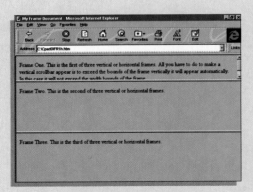

7 There's no text for this step but the author indicates a screen with text.

```
<HEAD>
<TITLE>My Frame Document</TITLE>
</HEAD>
<BODY>
```

2 In the <TITLE> area substitute New Page with My Frame Document.

```
<FRAMESET COLS="20%, *, *">
    <FRAME SRC="doc1.htm">
    <FRAME SRC="doc2.htm">
    <FRAME SRC="doc3.htm">
</FRAMESET>
```

3 Create the frameset (layout) page by moving the cursor to the space just after the <BODY> tag and typing in the text shown above.

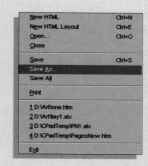

4 From the File menu select Save As and name the file FR1.htm in your CPad9 folder.

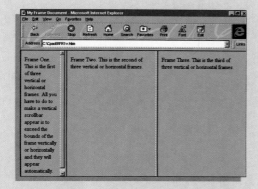

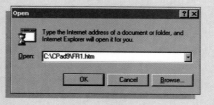

5 Restore your Internet Explorer from the Windows 95 Task bar and open the file you just made, FR1.htm. Viola! You have a page with three independent columns.

6 To create a page with three rows instead of three columns, use ROWS instead of COLS in the frameset tag: <FRAMESET ROWS="20%, *, *">. When you save the file and go back to Internet Explorer to view it, don't forget to refresh the screen.

How to Make Borderless and Complex Framesets

While it is nice to have frames that can represent different HTML files all on one page, they aren't of much use unless we can make them perform in the manner in which we designed the page. This is why we must initiate some control over our frameset pages with the tools we have acquired to this point.

Consider also how busy a page can get when we add a bunch of frames (the number is unlimited). To help alleviate this crowded looking condition, the Internet Explorer has the ability to view borderless frames. This is an IE exclusive which we will no doubt see in other browsers in the near future.

TIP SHEET

▶ Using borderless frames can clean up an otherwise cluttered page considerably. Many of Microsoft's Web pages contain borderless frames. For example, take a look at their home page at http://www.microsoft.com.

▶ When using borderless frames it is helpful to position the frames contents at the top left corner (normal position is slightly down and to the right). Change the individual frame page (in this case doc1.htm, doc2.htm, or doc3.htm) so its body tag includes the following: <BODY TOPMARGIN=0 LEFTMARGIN=0>.

▶ You can also create a frame using the Microsoft Forms 2.0 Frame control in the ActiveX Control Pad, but it allows no control over placement of the frame. The HTML Layout Control does not contain the Frames Control in its toolbox either. However, with just a little bit of HTML, you can create frames yourself.

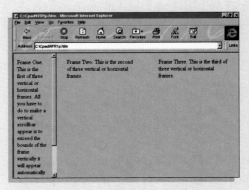

1 If you do not want viewers to be able to resize a frame you should add a NORESIZE attribute to the frame tag: <FRAME SRC= "doc1.htm" NORESIZE>.

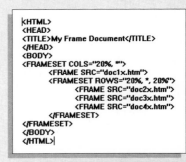

```
<HTML>
<HEAD>
<TITLE>My Frame Document</TITLE>
</HEAD>
<BODY>
<FRAMESET COLS="20%, *">
        <FRAME SRC="doc1x.htm">
        <FRAMESET ROWS="20%, *, 20%">
                <FRAME SRC="doc2x.htm">
                <FRAME SRC="doc3x.htm">
                <FRAME SRC="doc4x.htm">
        </FRAMESET>
</FRAMESET>
</BODY>
</HTML>
```

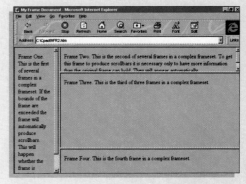

5 A more complex frameset might look like the following (shown with code and results). This is called nesting your frames.

If you do not want viewers to have scrollbars, you have to add a SCROLLING attribute to the frame tag and set it to "NO": <FRAME SRC= "doc1.htm" SCROLLING=NO>.

Frameset pages come with 3-D borders automatically. For an uncluttered seamless look, change the frameset tag to the following: <FRAMESET COLS="20%, *, *" FRAMEBORDER=0 FRAMESPACING=0>.

This screen contains borderless frames.

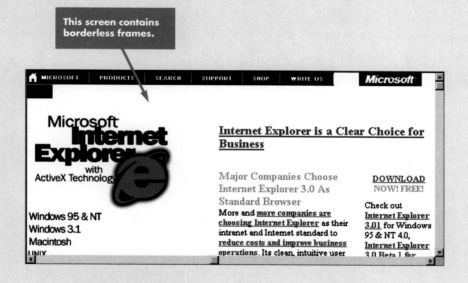

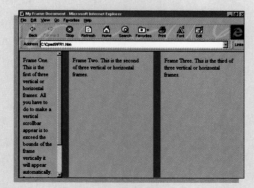

```
<HTML>
<HEAD>
<TITLE>My Frame Document</TITLE>
</HEAD>
<BODY BACKGROUND="picture.bmp">
<FRAMESET COLS="20%, *, *"FRAMEBORDER=0 FRAMESPACING=20>
    <FRAME SRC="doc1.htm"NORESIZE>
    <FRAME SRC="doc2.htm">
    <FRAME SRC="doc3.htm">
</FRAMESET>
</BODY>
</HTML>
```

```
<HTML>
<HEAD>
<TITLE>My Frame Document</TITLE>
</HEAD>
<BODY BGCOLOR="blue">
<FRAMESET COLS="20%, *, *"FRAMEBORDER=0 FRAMESPACING=20>
    <FRAME SRC="doc1.htm"NORESIZE>
    <FRAME SRC="doc2.htm">
    <FRAME SRC="doc3.htm">
</FRAMESET>
</BODY>
</HTML>
```

To place a colored or textured border between frames you need space between them, and you need to identify the background color or pattern. Add a Framespacing tag to your frameset document like one of these examples, and add the color and background specifications to the Body tag that's already there.

How to Use Floating Frames

A floating frame is similar to a window that floats in your page. Through the window you can see another Web page. Unlike regular frames that just rope off specific quadrants on a page, you can place an independent floating frame anywhere on a page. Thanks to margin-left and margin-right attributes you can position them anywhere. It all hinges on the <IFRAME> tag.

To make a floating frame, your first task is to create the page that will be seen in that window. Or, you can display someone else's Web site in your floating frame. However, for demonstration purposes we will use a local file in our CPad9 folder, C:\CPad9\local.htm. You'll find this file on the CD, where you can copy it to your CPad9 folder.

```
<HTML>
<HEAD>
<TITLE>My Floating Frames Document</TITLE>
</HEAD>
<BODY>
<IFRAME WIDTH=300 HEIGHT=75 FRAMEBORDER=0 SRC="local.htm">
        <FRAME WIDTH=300 HEIGHT=75 FRAMEBORDER=0 SRC="local.htm>
</IFRAME>
</BODY>
</HTML>
```

1 To create a floating frame using the ActiveX Control Pad, you have to insert it somewhere between the <BODY> tag and the </BODY> tag. Enter the copy for the IFRAME tag as shown here.

6 This last example shows how to target a floating frame with specific information or a Web site (code and results shown).

TIP SHEET

▶ In a similar fashion to stationary frames you can size floating frames using percentages rather than pixels. A sample IFRAME tag would look like this: <IFRAME WIDTH=40% HEIGHT=25% SRC="local.htm">.

▶ Use floating frames when you want a frame to remain visible on a page even though other frames change to other pages of Web sites.

2 Save the document in the CPad9 folder as FR3.htm.

3 Restore your Internet Explorer, open your FR3.htm, and view the results.

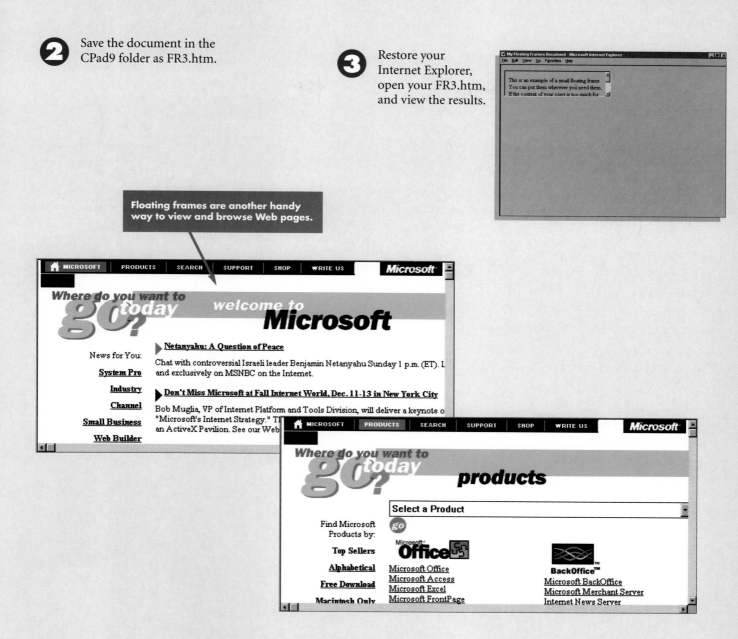

Floating frames are another handy way to view and browse Web pages.

5 Positioning a floating frame in an exact position is done like this (code example and results shown).

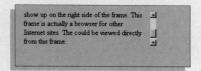

4 If you want to eliminate the border around your floating frame you can do so by adding the FRAMEBORDER attribute to the FRAMESET tag.

```
<BODY>
<IFRAME WIDTH=300 HEIGHT=75 FRAMEBORDER=0 SRC="local.htm">
    <FRAME WIDTH=300 HEIGHT=75 FRAMEBORDER=0 SRC="local.htm>
</IFRAME>
</BODY>
```

It's time to put the skills to work that you have learned in previous chapters. Your first exposure to Thunderbolt, Inc. was purely text-based; then we added a couple of simple controls. Now we will combine the text instrument along with frames, the HTML Layout Control, the Script Wizard, and even a few images. You will get more of an idea about just what the potential is for creating exciting Web pages.

Create a new directory called CPTry2. If you don't remember how to do this, go back to Chapter 1.

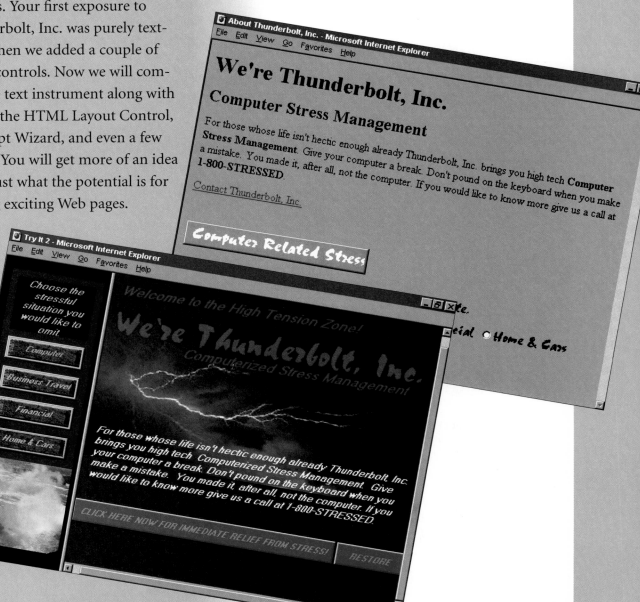

2 Start your ActiveX Control Pad and maximize your working area.

3 Begin your document by creating a simple frameset. On the line following the <BODY> tag type in the lines shown and change the Title to Try It 2.

4 Save the file as Exp1.htm in the CPpTry2 folder. Once opened, you can save most files by clicking on the disk icon in the toolbar.

5 From your ActiveX Control Pad open a new file, and save it as Cpad1.htm.

6 Place the cursor between the <BODY> and the </BODY> tags. Select the Edit menu and the Insert HTML Layout Control.

7 When the dialog box opens, name the new .alx file CPad1.alx. Click on OK.

8 A dialog box will appear asking if you want to create the file. Answer Yes.

9 You will see the .ALX object created instantly along with its icon. Click on the .ALX icon to edit this file.

Continue to next page ▶

TRY IT!

Continue below

12

You will need four CommandButtons. Double-click on the Command-Button icon in the toolbox, drag your cursor to your work area, and drag out the CommandButton four times. Clear the duplicator by clicking on a blank area of the toolbox and resize your CommandButtons so they are equal.

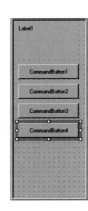

10

Your work area is supposed to fit in the first frame. Size it accordingly.

13

Place an Image area below the four CommandButtons and size it to fill the space. Click on the Image Control icon in the toolbox, and drag it in your work area to create the box.

11

Select the Label Control from the HTML Layout toolbox. Click on it and drag it to your work area. Make it into a box.

14

Place the cursor somewhere on the background of the layout and double-click to bring up its Properties window. Double-click on the BackColor property and select black. Click on OK.

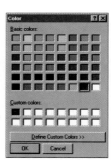

15

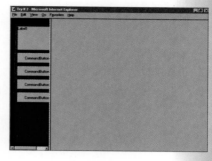

Switch to Internet Explorer and open the Exp1.htm file. You'll get an error message on the sage on the right side because we haven't created the Cpad2.htm file yet, but you can see the Cpad1.htm file on the left. Just ignore the error message, and notice that you can adjust its width by simply dragging the vertical bar to the right or left with your mouse.

16

Restore your ActiveX Control Pad. The chosen BackColor can be used to fill the area around the .alx file by changing the <BODY> tag in CPad1.htm to read <BODY BGCOLOR=black>.

17

Double-click on the blank Image Control to bring up the Properties window. Double-click on the PicturePath property and type in **C:\CPTry2\pic1.bmp**. Press Enter. Close the Properties window and resize the picture by dragging the handles inward.

18

Double-click on the Label box at the top of your Layout Control. In the Properties window double-click on BackColor and change it to black in the palette. Click on OK.

19

On the Caption property double-click and type in **Choose the stressful situation you would like to omit.** Press Enter. Double-click on Font and change it to Bold Italic and Size 10. To make the letters visible double-click ForeColor and choose yellow. Click OK. Double-click on the TextAlign property and choose 2-Center. Close the Properties window.

20

For each of the four CommandButton Controls perform the following steps: Double-click on the button and change each Caption to one of these four choices: **Computer; Business Travel; #Financial; Home & Cars.** Change the BackColor to yellow, the Font to Bold Italic, Picture property to **Marb1.bmp**, PicturePosition to 12-Center, and ForeColor to light blue. Close the Properties window and repeat for the next CommandButton.

Continue to next page ▶

TRY IT!

Continue below

21

Save the Layout (CPad1.alx) and then save the HTML document (CPad1.htm).

22

We want our CommandButtons to do something (actually take us to other URLs) when we click them, so highlight Command-Button1 with a click and open the Script Wizard by clicking on its icon.

23

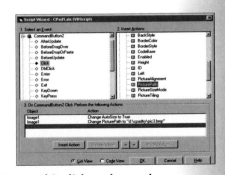

Click on the plus (+) next to Command-Button1 and then on the Click Event in the Events pane (left). We want this click to change the Image, so click on the plus (+) next to Image1 in the Actions pane (right). Double-click on AutoSize and OK (True). Double-click on PicturePath and enter D:\CPTry2\Pic2.bmp (your path) and click on OK. (For CommandButton2 it will be pic3.bmp, #3, pic4.bmp, and #4, pic5.bmp.)

24

Save your CPad1.alx file and close the .alx file. Save your CPad1.htm file, and for insurance save your Exp1.htm file.

25

For the other frame we will first return to the ActiveX Control Pad, and open a new file. Save it with the name **CPad2.htm**.

26

Place the cursor on the next line after the <BODY> tag. From the Menu bar select Edit and choose Insert HTML Layout.

27

When the dialog box pops up, name the new file **CPad2.alx** and click on Open. When asked if you wish to create this file answer Yes.

28

Click on the .ALX icon in the left margin to open the HTML Layout. Using your mouse to drag-and-drop borders, make your layout area approximately the size of your second frame.

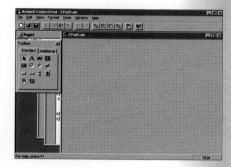

29

Click on the Image Control icon in the HTML Layout toolbox. From corner to corner drag your image box to fill your entire work area. Double-click anywhere inside your Image Control to bring out its Properties window. Double-click on the PicturePath property and enter the path **C:\CPTry2\ltpic1.gif**. Press Enter and then close the Properties window.

30

Double-click outside the picture to bring up the Properties window. Set the Back-Color to a shade compatible with the photo. Use "Define Custom Colors" and drag the arrow on the far right until the ColorSolid box is suitable to your eye. Click OK and close your Properties window.

31

From the toolbox grab four Label Controls, place them near the top, and size them to the width of the screen (you won't see them).

32

Double-click in the vicinity of the upper Label Control to bring out its Properties window. Double-click on Caption and type, **Welcome to the High Tension Zone!** Press Enter. Change the Font properties to Bold Italic and Size 14. BackStyle should be Transparent. Click OK. Change the ForeColor to a dusty green. Close the Properties window.

Continue to next page ▶

Continue
below

Double-click
on the next
Label
Control for
its Properties
window to
appear. The
Caption
property will be **We're Thunderbolt,
Inc.** The Font will be Shock (if not
available use MS Sans Serif, Italic),
Bold, and Size 35. Click OK. Change
the ForeColor to violet and exit the
Properties window.

Change the third Label's
Caption property to
**Computerized Stress
Management.**

On the
fourth Label
Control cre-
ate the body
copy similar
to that shown
in the illus-
tration.
Change the
properties of this box by first double-
clicking in the Label. Make the
BackStyle 0-Transparent, Font Italic,
Size 12, ForeColor white, and
WordWrap 1-True. Close the
Properties window to see the results.

36

Place one large Command-Button control beneath your type. First double-click its Properties window. Change the BackColor property to match the words, "Computerized Stress Management." Set the Caption property to "**CLICK HERE NOW FOR IMMEDIATE RELIEF FROM STRESS!**" Change the Font to Bold Italic and the ForeColor to bright green. Place a smaller CommandButton next to this one that reads **RESTORE**. Give it all the same properties as the larger one.

37

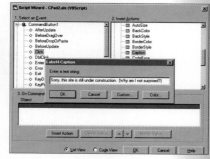

Click on one of the controls and open the script Wizard. In the events pane click on the plus (+) next to CommandButton1, and then on the Click Event. On the Actions side click on the plus (+) beside Label4. Double-click on its Caption property and enter **Sorry, this site is still under construction. (Why am I not surprised?)** Click OK.

38

Continue by changing the Font Name to **Shock** (if available), Size 18, ForeColor to an emerald green, TextAlign to 2-Center, and WordWrap to True.

39

Open the Script Wizard. In the Events pane click on the plus (+) beside CommandButton2 and then its Click Event. On the Actions side click on Label4. Change the Caption to read, **Contact 1-800-STRESSED for more information.** Make the Font Bold Italic, Size 16, and ForeColor to white. Click OK to exit.

40

Click on the disk icon to save the HTML Layout named CPad2.alx and close the Layout. Save CPad2.htm by clicking on the disk again.

41

Restore your Internet Explorer. In the Menu bar click on View and choose Refresh to see what you have wrought.

CHAPTER 10

How to Use Graphics in the ActiveX Control Pad

A good image can be worth a thousand words. Great images can make or break a Web site. In general there are two types of images we can use with the HTML Layout Control. Embedded images are used for any control that has a label. Stand-alone images are associated with the Image control.

Embedded images are used in an .alx (HTML Layout Control) file. Load an image into the Picture property on the proper control and the picture data is converted to a text format and stored in the HTML code of the .alx file. Usable picture formats include .bmp, .cur, .gif, .ico, .jpg, and .wmf. The Picture property is a great way to include a small picture on a label or button and avoid downloading a separate file.

Use stand-alone images with the Image control which has a Picture-Path property that can load .bmp, .gif, .jpg, and .wmf files. Using the PicturePath property is a good way to reduce the size of the .alx file, but it does require that the user download another file.

For this chapter you will create a directory and download some images into it from the CD, but you can also choose some images that you like from other sources.

How to Use Images

The use of images, pictures, and graphics has become the central issue when creating a Web site. Almost every part of a site can be image-oriented and it is important to remain within the boundaries of a well-planned theme for them to be effective. The images we created in the Try It section showed a few examples of image usage. This first section will get you set up for what follows.

We won't code anything unless we absolutely have to, so get your mouse ready to take wing.

▶ **1** Open your Windows Explorer and create a new directory called CPad10, and a subdirectory of that called Pix. Move all the image files for this chapter from the CD-ROM into the Pix directory so you can access them right from your hard drive. Keep everything from this chapter in the CPad10 directory.

TIP SHEET

▶ **Page painting performance or Web page performance can be improved by using the HTML Layout Control to set the DrawBuffer property when the page is run. The value of DrawBuffer is the number of pixels reserved for off-screen painting. Increasing the value of DrawBuffer will let you paint large controls more quickly, but will let you use more memory. Large images will have problems unless you increase the value of DrawBuffer.**

▶ **Images can be used as general graphics to gain attention of the viewer. Use them to enlighten, explain, enthuse, and entertain.**

▶ **Images can be used for a subtle or striking background to a Web page. It depends on the subject matter, but the subtle graphic definitely has its place.**

▶ **Images can be used as banners or rules to divide portions of a page.**

▶ **Use images in conjunction with a CommandButton, HotSpot, or other control to navigate from page to page, section to section, or move to another Web site.**

2 From the Edit menu select Insert HTML Layout and place it after the <BODY> tag in the HTML template. Name the file CPTen1.alx and place it in your CPad10 directory.

3 Click on the .ALX icon in the left margin to open the HTML Layout Control. Maximize your work area and you are ready to create images for your page.

Coordinated Web site graphics pages from the Microsoft Internet Explorer Multimedia Gallery

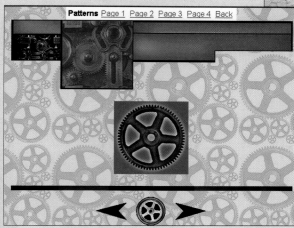

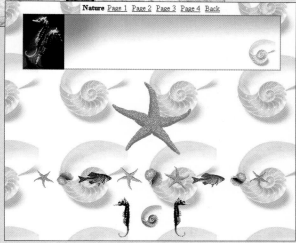

How to Create Overlapping Images

It has become very common to put one image in front of another on a Web page. A variety of interesting effects can be reached by layering controls using z-order, loading new images, and setting the Visible property of the Image control. Z-order is the order in which the images were created. It can be changed with toolbar icons in the ActiveX Control Pad.

▶ **1** Open your ActiveX Control Pad and your CPTen1.alx file in the HTML Layout Control.

7 Try all the same things with four photo images (pic1.bmp, pic2.bmp, pic3.bmp, and pic4.bmp). The same rules apply for photos as for clip art images.

6 As long as one of the Image controls is highlighted, the z-order tools in the toolbar will be activated. From left to right you can use these tools to Bring to Front, Move Forward, Move Backward, and Send to Back.

2 Double-click on the Image Control icon. Place four fairly equal controls on your Layout. To cancel the duplicating feature, move the cursor to a blank area in the toolbox and click once.

3 Double-click on one of the Image controls to bring out the Properties window. Enter the PicturePath property for the clip art graphic of a boat (D:\CPad10\Pix\boat.wmf, for example) and press Enter. Drag the graphic down to a small size. Exit the Properties window.

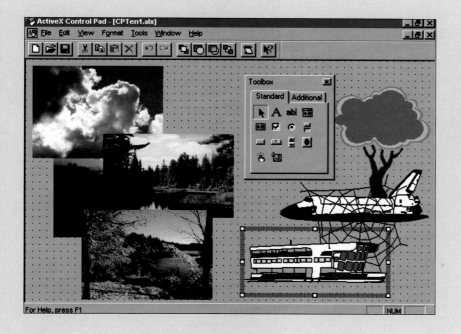

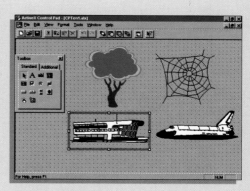

4 Do the same for the other three Image controls you have created, using the graphics shuttle.wmf, then spidrweb.wmf, then tree.wmf. Now you should have four separate images.

5 Use your mouse to move the images so they overlap. The tree was created last and can be overlapped by anything, the shuttle can be overlapped by the spiderweb and the boat, and the spiderweb can be overlapped by the boat only. Nothing can overlap the boat because it was created first. This is known as the z-order.

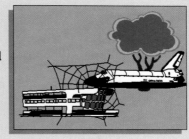

How to Create a Background Image

A full background image and a tiled background image are the two simple types of backgrounds you can make. Unless you need a big flashy background image to clarify a particular point, a more subtle tiled background image will be the most efficient. It will load quickly and it won't detract from the main content of your page. Always be careful that your background image doesn't make your text hard to read.

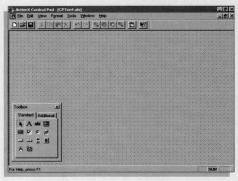

▶ ❶ Open your ActiveX Control Pad and the HTML Layout control for CPTen1.htm (and CPTen1.alx). Maximize your Layout area.

❽ Save your .alx file, close your Layout control, and save your HTML file. Restore your Internet Explorer and click on Refresh.

❼ Restore your ActiveX Control Pad and reopen your .alx file. Double-click somewhere on the image. Change the PictureSizeMode to 0-Clip and PictureTiling to 1-True. Exit the Properties window. You've just changed your full background into a tiled background.

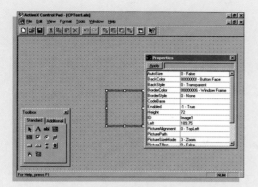

2 Select the Image control icon and click once. Place an Image control in an open area. Double-click inside the Image control box that appears on the screen to get its Properties window.

3 Double-click on the PicturePath property and enter the path for the desired graphic. Press Enter.

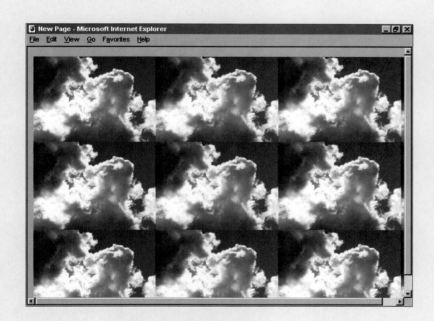

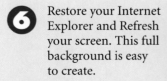

6 Restore your Internet Explorer and Refresh your screen. This full background is easy to create.

4 Drag the picture to the extreme upper left corner of the layout. Then drag the lower right handle down and to the right. Save the layout after closing the Properties window.

5 Close the Layout (.alx file) and save the HTML (ActiveX Control Pad) file.

How to Use Transparent Images

Transparent images are those that allow you to see underlying images or text. An opaque image has a white or colored background.

Embedded images (for any control that has a label) are always transparent. Either the file format provides this transparency, or the HTML Layout Control will provide transparency. Stand-alone transparent images work only with the Image control.

Transparency is completely dependent on the file format. For instance, the .jpg format does not support transparency but the .gif does.

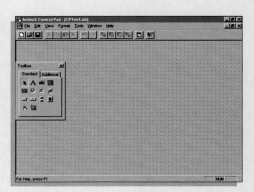

▶ **1** Restore your ActiveX Control Pad and open your CPTen1.alx (layout) file.

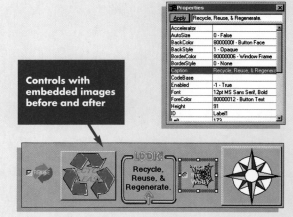

Controls with embedded images before and after

7 You will probably want to add captions to some of the controls. For any of the controls, open the Properties window and double-click on the Caption property. Type in your new Caption and press Enter, then change the PicturePosition property to 12-Center. If you still don't see the caption, try changing the ForeColor property to a lighter color.

2 Use the toolbox to create a couple of Image controls. Double-click on one of the controls to bring up a Properties window. Enter a path in the PicturePath property and click Enter. Repeat this for the other Image control.

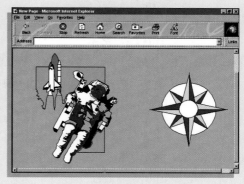

3 Images created by using the Image control with a PicturePath or URL are examples of stand-alone transparent images. Any image created with an Image control is transparent by default.

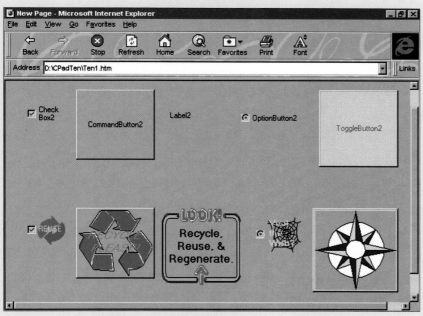

4 When you load an image in the Picture property of a Checkbox, CommandButton, Label, OptionButton, or ToggleButton, you have examples of embedded images. Using the HTML Layout Toolbox create a blank control for each of the aforementioned.

5 Double-click on each of these controls to introduce the Properties window, double-click on the Picture property, and supply the file name for picture in the PicturePath property. Pick a picture from the dialog box. Click Open.

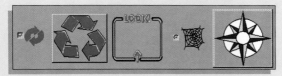

6 When the picture appears in your control you may want to grab the handles and size it to fit your control. Repeat this for each of your five controls.

How to Create a Changeable Image

Long ago the general computing population decided it wanted images to do the work. Here is how you can make your images into hyperlinks, so they can drive your Web site navigation.

▶ **1** Open a new page on your ActiveX Control Pad. Select the Edit menu and choose Insert HTML Layout. Supply the name for this Layout (CPTen2.alx) and click on Open.

6 In the toolbox click on the "hand" and place a small box around the sun in the Image control.

5 (D:\CPad10\Pix\pic3.bmp). Place a Label beneath the picture in which the Caption reads, Click on the Sun to close the box.

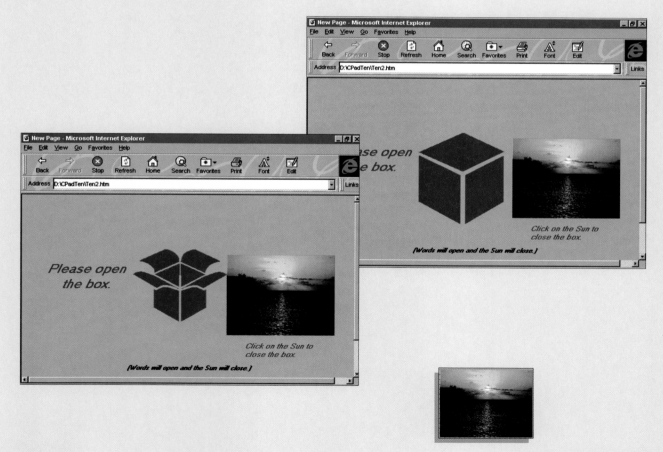

2 Click on the .ALX icon to open the HTML Layout Control. Maximize your working area. From the toolbox drag out an Image control and a Label control (shown shaded here so they are visible).

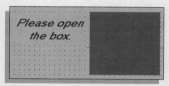

3 Double-click on the Label control. In the Properties window double-click on the Caption property and type in Please open the box. Press Enter. Change the Font to Bold Italic and Size 18. Change ForeColor to blue, MousePointer to 2-Cross, TextAlign to 2-Center. Close the Properties window.

4 To the right of the Image control drag out another Image control. Double-click it and change the PicturePath to bring in a picture

How to Create a Changeable Image (Continued)

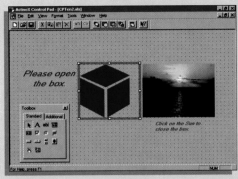

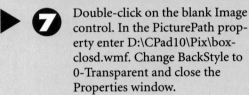

▶ **7** Double-click on the blank Image control. In the PicturePath property enter D:\CPad10\Pix\box-closd.wmf. Change BackStyle to 0-Transparent and close the Properties window.

12 Restore your Internet Explorer and open the Ten2.htm file. When you move the cursor to "Please open the box," or when you move the cursor to the Sun, notice it changes to a cross. You now can open and close the box.

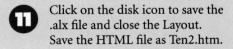

11 Click on the disk icon to save the .alx file and close the Layout. Save the HTML file as Ten2.htm.

8 With one of the controls highlighted, open the Script Wizard by clicking on its icon. Click on the plus (+) next to Label1 in the Events pane and select the Click Event (with a click). On the Actions side click on the plus (+) next to Image1. Double-click on PicturePath and enter D:\CPad10\Pix\boxopen.wmf.

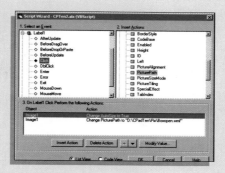

9 Click on the plus (+) next to HotSpot1 in the Events pane and select the Click Event. On the Actions side click on the plus (+) beside Image1. Double-click on PicturePath and enter D:\CPad10\Pix \boxclosd.wmf. Click OK to close the Script Wizard.

10 For informational purposes only, place another label beneath the controls that reads Words will open and the Sun will close.

How to Create Horizontal Rules

With HTML code it is easy to produce a plain horizontal rule with the <HR> tag. However, you cannot simply insert this tag in an HTML Layout.

There are many ways to create custom horizontal rules, if you don't like the plain ones provided by regular HTML. Use a drawing or paint program to produce the graphic you'll use (or use one of those provided on the CD), then place it on your pages using the HTML Layout Control.

▶ **1** Assuming a central theme (sunset) is found, choose a picture or central graphic that has bright color or good contrast (CPad10\Pix\pic3.bmp).

6 Click Edit and click on Paste two more times. Place the two new images on either side of the original bar. Even though the horizontal bar will have to be moved in three separate pieces, you do have a quick and effective horizontal bar to use. The example of this is saved in CPTen3.alx and Ten3.htm

2 In the ActiveX Control Pad open a new HTML Layout control and name it CPTen3.alx. Place an Image control on the Layout with the PicturePath property changed to C:\CPad10\Pix\pic3.bmp. Place a Label control just beneath the full size picture you have chosen. You are limited by the original size of the picture.

3 Double-click in the Label area to get to its properties. In the Caption delete the word Label1 and press Enter. Open the Picture property with a double-click and choose the same graphic image as you used before. Click on Open.

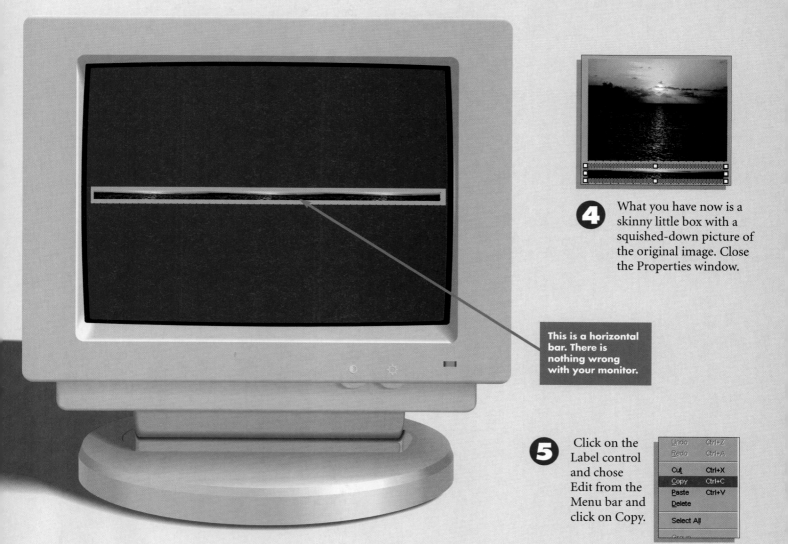

4 What you have now is a skinny little box with a squished-down picture of the original image. Close the Properties window.

This is a horizontal bar. There is nothing wrong with your monitor.

5 Click on the Label control and chose Edit from the Menu bar and click on Copy.

CHAPTER 11

How to Create Images and Graphics

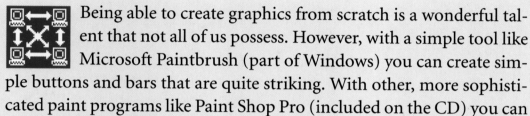Being able to create graphics from scratch is a wonderful talent that not all of us possess. However, with a simple tool like Microsoft Paintbrush (part of Windows) you can create simple buttons and bars that are quite striking. With other, more sophisticated paint programs like Paint Shop Pro (included on the CD) you can resort to tricks and magic to create really impressive navigational elements, subtle backgrounds, and stunning typography.

Using existing images, clip art, and photos will get you off to a great start when creating graphics for Web sites. When looking for images, remember that the file formats supported by the ActiveX Control Pad and the HTML Layout control collectively are .bmp, .wmf, .jpg, and .gif. Be aware that any photo or graphic automatically has a copyright, whether it carries a copyright symbol or not. Don't scan or steal copyrighted materials and publish them on your Web page.

How to Make Buttons with Microsoft Paintbrush

It is common to use buttons to navigate from page to page in a Web site. They can be any shape or color. They may even contain a photo or logo. It is also advantageous to divide important areas of a Web site with horizontal bars. In the HTML Layout control these can take the form of an Image control or a Label control.

▶ **1** Before we get started, the first thing we need is a place to keep the graphics we are going to be building. On your choice of drives create a new folder in Windows Explorer named CPad11.

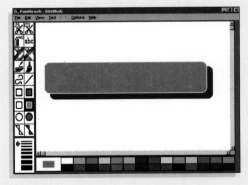

6 If you want to do a shaded effect using Windows Paintbrush, select the shadow color you want first, then the shape you want. Drag out your shadow area. Then change the color to be the button color, and drag out a second similar shape over the first, but a little offset from it. This is easy with just a little practice. If you want to create a plain bar simply drag it out horizontally and reduce the height to a minimum.

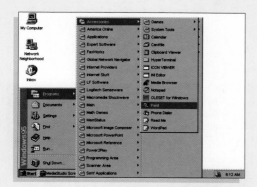

2 Start the Windows Paintbrush program by clicking on Start, selecting Programs, then Accessories, and finally Paint.

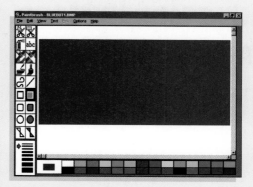

3 Buttons and bars can be solid or open depending upon your choice from the toolbox. Select the blue on the color bar and solid box on the toolbar. Drag out a rectangular button on your screen.

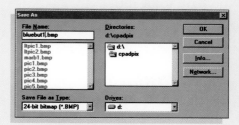

4 From the File menu click on Save As. In the Save As dialog box locate your CPad11 folder. Name your file Bluebut1.bmp and click on OK.

5 When you are in the ActiveX Control Pad using your HTML Layout Control, place the button in the Picture property of a Label control. From there you can size it and place it wherever you wish.

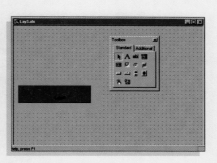

How to Create Advanced Buttons and Button Bars

Microsoft Paintbrush is adequate as a very basic graphics tool. However, for more professional looking graphical representations you need to have the versatility of a real paint program like Paint Shop Pro 4.0, which is on the CD. As you will soon find out, this is a great program for customizing graphics.

If you haven't already installed this program on your hard drive, you need to run psp.exe from the CD. Paint Shop Pro (http://www.jasc .com) will guide you through the entire installation. Once installed, you may run the program immediately.

Paint Shop Pro provides you with a great variety of combinations of effects. Experiment and have some fun.

TIP SHEET

▶ With various special effects, filters, and deformations you have an unlimited number of effects that are possible with Paint Shop Pro. Have fun trying all the various combinations.

▶ If you don't have a CD-ROM drive you can easily download the Shareware version of Paint Shop Pro from the Web site, http://www.jasc.com.

▶ Shareware software has a limited free trial period. After your trial expires you must either delete the software from your computer or pay a registration fee to the company that developed the program.

 1 Start the Paint Shop Pro program. To start a new image click on File and then New. A box will appear in which you can select

size and background color. Let's start with a bar. A good size is 900 x 30 pixels with a background color of white. Click OK.

10 Use the Edit menu to Copy and Paste one more of the same button, calling it ButtonDn. For the button on the right select Image and Mirror from the Menu bar to turn it around. You now have two-color coordinated buttons to use in a Web site, one of which is pressed in. Once again, you can make these buttons "hot" for navigation by using the HotSpot control, OptionButton, or other click-type ActiveX control.

9 Save the image as ButtonUp.gif.

8 In the Buttonize window you can now adjust the size of your edges by percentage and whether you want the Transparent or Solid image (transparent buttons have smooth edges and solid are sharp lines where the edges drop off). Click OK.

7 Select Image on the Menu bar, Special Effects, and Buttonize.

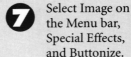

2 When the blank image box appears, your next move is to go to the color palette. As you move the mouse over the color palette, notice that the color in the lower box continually changes. Select your primary color by clicking with the left mouse button and your secondary color by clicking with your right mouse button.

3 In the Fill style box at the top of the page select Sunburst Gradient. Use the Flood Fill icon and click in the blank area of your control.

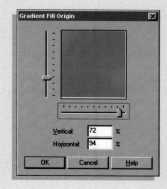

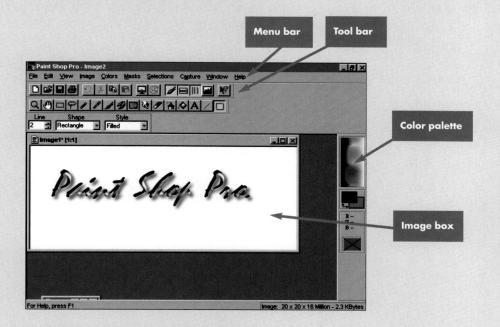

4 Select the Flood Fill icon in the toolbar with your mouse. Move the cross part of the icon into your image box and click once. You will then have a Sunburst Gradient bar.

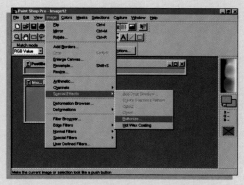

6 To produce a button with similar characteristics you do not have to change the colors. From the Menu bar select File and New again. Size the image at 100 x 100 with a white Background color. Move your Flood Fill icon to the new image box and click on it once. You would do this if you needed to create other shapes and sizes of button in the same color scheme.

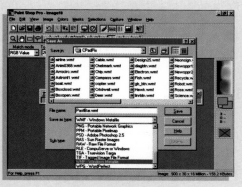

5 Select File and Save As from the Menu bar. When the Save As dialog box pops up select .GIF (a format supported by most browsers) and name the file PastlBar.gif. Click on Save.

How to Change a Picture into a Button

Changing a picture into a button can be one of the easiest things you can do to improve a Web site. It is also a great trick for creating a coordinated Web site.

▶ **1** From the File menu in Paint Shop Pro, select Open. Then select a picture you would like to see as a button. Use CPad11\busplane.bmp for this exercise.

8 Then choose Image, Special Effects, Buttonize with a Solid edge.

7 Choose Image, Special Filters, Emboss.

2 Select Image, Special Effects, and Buttonize from the Menu bar. How easy can it get?

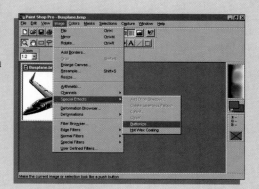

3 Adjustments may be made in the Buttonize window for the height of the button (edges by percentage) and whether the button is transparent (rounded edges) or solid (sharp cut edges). Click OK.

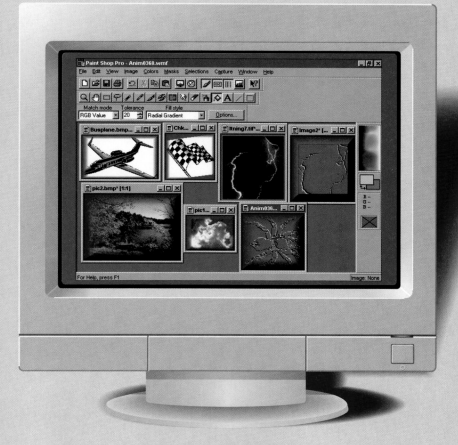

4 Save your button and try some variations in the Buttonize window.

6 Add a border by selecting Image, Add Borders.

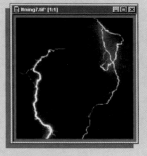

5 Now try it with a picture. Select a picture from the CD or from the CPadPix folder. Use the Menu bar, File, Open, (use pic2.bmp) and OK.

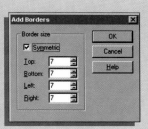

How to Create Great Drop Shadow Effects

One of the most dramatic things you can do to type is to add a drop shadow effect. Here's how you can do it with a minimum amount of effort, using Paint Shop Pro.

▶ **1** In Paint Shop Pro select File and New from the Menu bar. In the New Image dialog box select a size for your Image box. For this exercise use 300 x 100 with a white Background color. Click OK.

2 In the color palette use the left mouse button to select your primary color, which will show up as the color of your type. You must select the color you want before you select the type. The secondary color (right mouse button) will become the color of your drop shadow.

3 Click on the Text icon (the capital A) in the toolbar. Then move your cursor to the image area and click once. The Add Text window will appear. Select Shock (if available), Size 24, and enter the text in the pane provided at the bottom, Thunderbolt, Inc. Click OK.

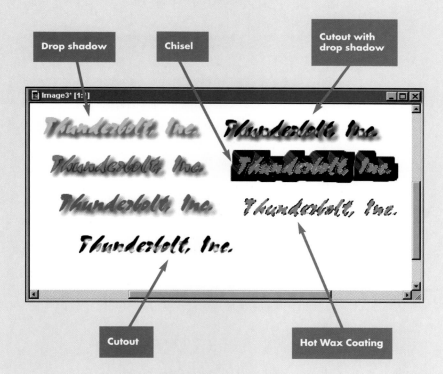

Drop shadow

Chisel

Cutout with drop shadow

Cutout

Hot Wax Coating

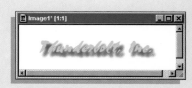

4 To introduce the drop shadow click on Image, Special Effects, Add Drop Shadow. Manipulate your shadow effect from this dialog box and click OK.

5 Other Special Effects include Cutout (Image, Special Effects, Cutout); Cutout with Drop Shadow (Cutout plus Drop Shadow); Chisel (Image, Special Effects, Chisel); Buttonize (you already know that); and Hot Wax Coating. All are located in the SpecialEffects menu.

How to Create Muted and Embossed Backgrounds

When you use background images, it's important that your images be low contrast so they don't interfere with the foreground of your page. High-quality paint programs like Adobe PhotoShop or Paint Shop Pro make creating these images easy.

▶ **1** In Paint Shop Pro, your first step in creating an embossed background is getting a picture. Use the file menu, select Open, and get a picture CPad11\CPadPix\jeff.bmp.

8 To mute the picture more increase the %Brightness.

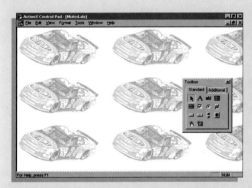

7 If you wish to use a muted or soft image instead of the embossed one you can just save the image from step 3 of this exercise and pick up again at step 6.

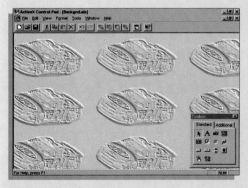

6 Change the PictureSizeMode property to 0-Clip and PictureTiling to 1-True. Close the Properties window and drag the picture to the far upper left portion of the Layout. Drag the lower right image handle down and to the right until you run out of screen. Voila! A tiled and embossed background.

2 Lower the contrast by selecting Colors on the Menu bar, Adjust, and Brightness/Contrast. Increase the %Brightness to 35 and decrease the %Contrast to 0. Click OK.

3 From the Image Menu choose Special Filters and select Emboss. Repeat step 2 of this exercise.

Tiled Image / Embossed

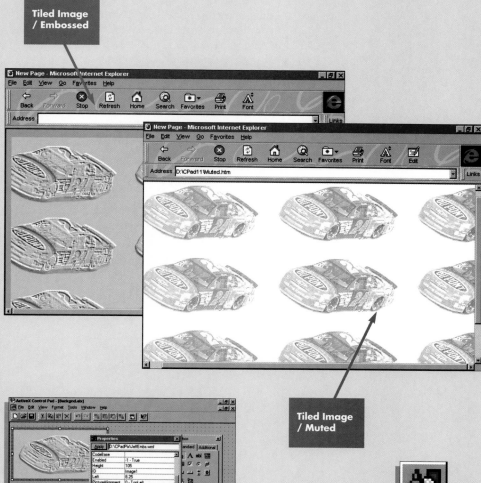

Tiled Image / Muted

4 Save the image in .bmp, .jpg, .wmf, or .gif format. Reopen or Restore your ActiveX Control Pad. Within the <BODY> tags of the blank HTML document insert an HTML Layout control (Edit, Insert HTML Layout). Save it in the CPad11 file folder, and name it Backgnd.alx. Open the Layout with a click on the .ALX icon.

5 Maximize your Layout. Drag an Image control (click on Image icon) to the upper left corner of the screen and click once. Double-click within the boundaries of the blank Image control. In the Properties window that appears double-click on the PicturePath property and enter the path where you stored the embossed image.

TRY IT!

Graphics and image implementation can be one of the most time-consuming parts of Web page production. However, by using existing artwork and the HTML Layout Control, your development time can be radically cut. What you will be doing here is to take an existing frameset (three vertical frames) and fill each one with graphics and controls. In frame 1 you will place a set of overlapping transparent images. This is great for display purposes or online brochures. Frame 2 will house a grouping of clickable images. Click on each of the three in the control and the main graphic will change (as described in Chapter 8 these could also take you to a completely different URL at some other location). The controls you create in Frame 3 will change the text in the "Look" box. The image manipulation you are learning here will assist you later in navigating from site to site or among your own pages. It's time to try your hand at this.

For this exercise a simple frameset was developed for you that is located in the CPTry3 folder on the CD. For best results, copy this folder and its contents to your hard drive using the Windows Explorer. Open CPTry3A.htm in the ActiveX Control Pad. Open the same file in your Internet Explorer. You will see the two views of the frameset files you will be working with.

Minimize the size of your CPTry3.htm file in the ActiveX Control Pad and you will see the four pages that make up your frameset.

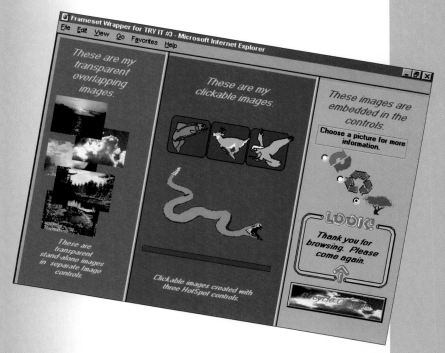

Maximize CPTry3A.htm. Click on the .ALX icon to open the first frame Layout control.

Maximize your Layout. Click on the View menu and then on the toolbar and status bar to have as clean a layout area as possible. This file controls 30% of the Web page along the left side. Double-click anywhere on the layout and change the BackColor property (double-click) to olive green. Click OK and exit the Properties window.

Double-click on the label This is CPTry3A.htm. Change the BackStyle property to 0-Transparent, the Caption to **These are my transparent overlapping images,** and press Enter. Change the Font to Bold Italic, Size 12; ForeColor to bright yellow (John Deere would be proud); and TextAlign to 2-Center. Close the Properties window.

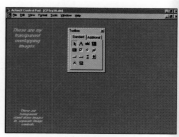

From the toolbox drag another label control and place it near the bottom of the Layout. This one will read **These are transparent stand-alone images in separate Image controls.** All the properties should be the same as those in Step 5, except Font Size will be 10.

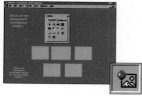

Double-click on the Image Control icon in the toolbox, move over to the Layout and click five times. You just created five Image controls (turn off the duplicating feature by pointing to a blank area in the Toolbox and clicking once). For the time being, change the BackStyle property to Opaque for each of the controls so you can find them. Move them all where you can see them plainly.

Double-click on one of the Image controls, and then double-click on the PicturePath property. Enter the path for the picture: C:\CPTry3\Pix\pic1.bmp. Press Enter. Drag the picture down to a small enough size to use for this exercise. Be sure to change the BackStyle property back to Transparent (now you can see it). Check the illustration here for a size reference.

Perform the same steps for the other four Image controls and use **pic2.bmp, pic3.bmp, pic4.bmp,** and **pic5.bmp** in each PicturePath property.

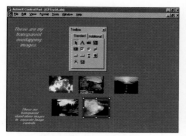

When you've got all five pictures in their Image controls you can drag-and-drop those controls in place between the two Label controls. Arrange them until you are satisfied with the result.

Continue to next page ▶

TRY IT!

Continue below

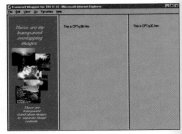

11

Save the Layout, close the Layout, and save the HTML document. Restore your Internet Explorer and Refresh the screen.

12

On to the center frame. From your ActiveX Control Pad click File on the Menu bar, then Open. Open CPTry3B.htm.

13

Click on the .ALX icon to open your HTML Layout Control for the center frame. Maximize your Layout and double-click anywhere in the frame to get its Properties window. Double-click on BackColor and choose the sea green at the bottom of the palette. Close the Properties window.

14

Double-click on the Label in the upper left corner of the layout. Make the BackStyle 0-Transparent, with a Caption reading These are my clickable images. Press Enter. Change the Font to Bold Italic, Size 12, and the ForeColor to the lighter shade of yellow. Make the TextAlign property 2-center and exit the Properties window. Fit the Label in the middle of the center frame.

15

Drag out another Label control from the toolbox and place it near the bottom of the frame. Double-click on it and set the properties to BackStyle 0-Transparent, set the Caption to Clickable images created with three HotSpot controls, set the Font to Bold Italic, set the ForeColor to the same lighter yellow, and set the TextAlign to 2-Center. Close the Properties window.

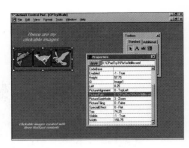

16

Click on the Image control icon and drag it beneath the top Label. Double-click on the new control to show its Properties. Double-click on the PicturePath property and enter the path for the picture, C:\CPTry3\Pix\Wildlife.wmf. Press Enter and close the Properties window.

Double-click on the HotSpot icon in the Toolbox and put a HotSpot on each of the three pictures of the fish, deer, and hawk. Although you only have one image control, a HotSpot can overlay any part of the control (in this case three HotSpots do the trick). Click in a blank area of the Toolbox to shut off the duplication feature.

Double-click on the first HotSpot and make the MousePointer property 2-Cross. Do this for each of the three HotSpot controls. Close the Properties window.

 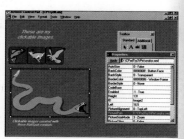

Place another image beneath the first (use the Image icon from the Toolbox). Double-click on the Image and enter the PicturePath C:\CPTry3\Pix\snake.wnf.

Put in a horizontal bar by dragging in a skinny label from the Toolbox. Double-click on the Label control and set the BackColor to blue, the BorderStyle to 1-Single, and delete the words in the Caption property. Close the Properties window.

Save the Layout, close the screen, save the HTML document, restore your Internet Explorer, click on View (Menu bar), and Refresh. Make a note of any adjustments you might wish to make and reopen your ActiveX Control Pad and current HTML Layout control.

 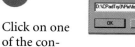 

Click on one of the controls to highlight it and open the Script Wizard (Tools on the Menu bar). Click on the plus (+) sign next to HotSpot1 and then select the Click Event. Move to the Actions pane and click on the plus (+) sign beside the Image2 control. In the Actions pane double-click on the Picture-Path. Since HotSpot1 is on the fish, enter the path C:\CPTry3\Pix\fish.wmf. Click OK.

Continue to next page ▶

TRY IT!

**Continue
below**

23

Without leaving the Script Wizard, perform the same task for HotSpot2 (deer.wmf) and HotSpot3 (hawk.wmf). Also do the same using Label3 (the blue horizontal bar) as a control to restore Image2 to snake.wmf. When complete click OK to close the Script Wizard.

24

Save the Layout, close the Layout, save the HTML document, restore your Internet Explorer, Refresh the screen, and try out the controls for frame 2 and frame 3 by clicking on them.

25

Go back to the ActiveX Control pad and open the CPTry3C.htm file.

26

Click on the .ALX icon to open and maximize the HTML Layout control for frame 3.

27

Double-click anywhere on the Layout. Change the BackColor property to a light blue. Click OK.

28

For the label at the top change the BackStyle property to 0-Transparent; the Caption to read These images are embedded in the controls; the Font to Bold Italic and Size 12; ForeColor to burgundy; and TextAlign to 2-Center. Close the Properties window and adjust the control so the type will fit.

29

Below the label add a second label control, three OptionButton controls (stacked), an Image control with a TextBox inside it, and a CommandButton on the bottom. (And a partridge in a pear tree.)

30

Change the properties as listed for these controls: Label2: BackStyle 0-Transparent, BorderStyle 1-Single, BorderColor red, Caption **Choose a picture for more information**, Font Bold, TextAlign 2-Center. OptionButton1: BackStyle 0-Transparent, Caption blank, Picture arrocirc.wmf OptionButton2: Backstyle 0-Transparent, Caption blank, Picture recycle.wmf OptionButton3: BackStyle 0-Transparent, Caption blank, Picture tree.wmf Image1: PicturePath D:\CPadTry3\Pix\neonsign.wmf TextBox1: BackStyle 0-Transparent, BorderStyle 0-None, TextAlign 2-Center CommandButton1: Caption Recycle Contents, Font Bold Italic Size 10, Picture pic1.bmp, PicturePosition 12-Center, ForeColor red.

31

Click on one of the controls to make it active then open the Script Wizard once again.

32

Let's move from the top to the bottom on our Layout. In the Events pane click on the plus(+) sign next to OptionButton1 and select the Click Event. We want it to change the TextBox so we click on the plus (+) sign beside TextBox1 in the Actions pane. Double-click on Text and type Reuse containers whenever you get the chance. Click OK. Set the Font to Bold Italic and Size 10.

33

Perform the same for OptionButton2 except we want it to read Recycle today for a better World tomorrow.(Text). The Text for OptionButton3 will be Plant a tree so we all can breathe easier.

34

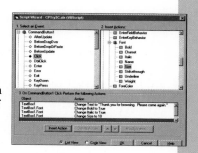

For Command Button1 create the Click Event in the Events side of the Script Wizard. On the Actions side (TextBox1) the Font should be changed to Bold Italic and Size 10, and the Text should be Thank you for browsing. Click OK to close the Script Wizard.

35

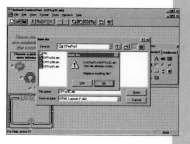

Save the Layout and close the .alx file. Save the HTML code also.

36

Restore your Internet Explorer and Refresh the screen.

37

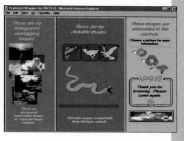

Test all the controls. If no adjustments are needed then you are finished with the exercise.

CHAPTER 12

How to Make Your Graphics Work for You

 All this talk of graphics, their creation and their use would be pointless if we didn't tell you how to put it all together. Start out by moving the CPad12 folder and its contents from the CD to your hard drive.

In this chapter we'll help you with proper use of graphics (and in this case their ActiveX controls) in the form of backgrounds, headers, photos, buttons, bars, typeface, and so forth. The combination of carefully selected images with the use of ActiveX controls is a great way to find optimal solutions for your objectives.

Approach every item on a Web page as though it were an image. With the use of the HTML Layout Control and its toolbox, any item or group of items can be used to create a response in your viewer's mind.

Remember that we're not using HTML to hard code these elements. We are using ActiveX controls, the methods they support, and the properties they embrace. The advantages of using the ActiveX Control Pad over straight HTML are its built-in features of flexibility, ease of use, and automatic code generation with the Script Wizard.

How to Design an Eye-Catching Web Site

Let's look at the four E's for Web page design. Our images must explain, enlighten, encourage, and entertain. Here we'll examine the parts of a Web page and each element therein as created with the ActiveX Control Pad and the HTML Layout control.

1 Background images add life to Web pages. They add texture, personality, and color to an otherwise mundane environment. We can place backgrounds using the Image control.

2 A graphical banner can be every bit as strong a statement as a text headline. A good banner can meet or exceed all of the four E's. Place your banner with an Image control.

10 Navigation buttons take you to other pages within this site, and are repeated on each page in the site so that your viewer won't get "lost" in your pages. Use Label, Image, and HotSpot controls to create navigation buttons.

9 On commercial sites you will often see an advertisement for the services of the creating company or of paid advertisers. Viewers can jump to other sites that might be of interest with these links. Check with your service provider first if you want to use advertising on your page, which you can place with a combination of Label, Image, and HotSpot controls.

8 Very often the Web page creator's e-mail address will be included on a page so that viewers may send comments to the site builder. Use a Label control with a HotSpot control over it to include your e-mail address on your pages.

TIP SHEET

▸ **If you want the code for an image to be included in the .alx (HTML Layout) portion of your HTML document, you should use a Label control. The Image control will specify a path for finding the image, but the image isn't part of the document.**

▸ **A well designed Web page will fit on the screen with little or no scrolling. Everything your viewer needs initially should be readily available in that small space.**

▸ **Small tidbits of information are more easily digested than huge mouthfuls. Keep information as brief as possible.**

▸ **This page contains 23 ActiveX controls. Most of the images are from the Microsoft Internet Explorer Multimedia Gallery. "Nature Needs Help!" and "Dangerous Ideas" were created with Paint Shop Pro.**

3 The title or headline should be another attention getter. Use an Image or Label control to place this element.

4 Body copy should be both attractive and readable. It is there to explain, clarify, and pose creative situations. Place your body text with one or more Label or TextBox controls.

5 A horizontal rule or bar is used to divide portions of a page. It can break the flow of the text for better readability. Use the Image control to position your horizontal rules.

6 Vendor or support logos can be very helpful and add visual interest. Including names that people know and respect adds credibility to a Web site. These graphics are often a direct link to the company's Web site, and are positioned with the Image and Hotspot controls.

7 Hypertext combines text and the HotSpot control. Click on this text and you will go directly to the the linked Web site.

Home page anatomy
Does this Home page meet the standards?
  Explanation
  Enlightenment
  Encouragement
  Entertainment

Background
(Image control)

Banner
(Image control)

Title or headline
(Image or Label control)

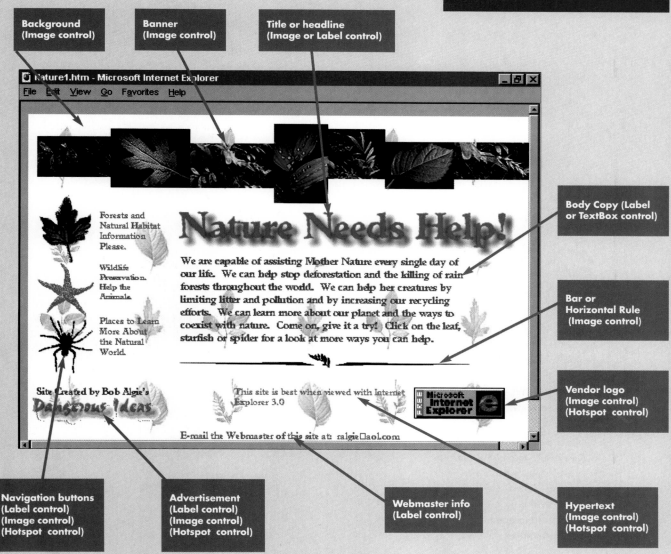

Body Copy (Label
or TextBox control)

Bar or
Horizontal Rule
(Image control)

Vendor logo
(Image control)
(Hotspot control)

Navigation buttons
(Label control)
(Image control)
(Hotspot control)

Advertisement
(Label control)
(Image control)
(Hotspot control)

Webmaster info
(Label control)

Hypertext
(Image control)
(Hotspot control)

How to Make Your Pages Large Enough to Fit Your Images

It is difficult to create a Web page with everything you want on it (including anchovies), all in one HTML Layout. Here's how to use multiple HTML Layouts to create all the room you will ever need.

1 In your ActiveX Control Pad, open your saved **Nature1.alx** file. Choose Edit on the Menu bar and open a second .alx file just below that one. Use the new file name **Nature1b.alx**.

7 Open or Restore your Internet Explorer and Open the Nature1a.htm file. Compare the results of the single page and the extended HTML documents.

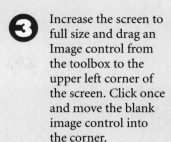

2 Click on the .ALX icon to open the new Layout and change the BackColor property to white. (Remember the Properties window is just a double-click away.) Click OK.

3 Increase the screen to full size and drag an Image control from the toolbox to the upper left corner of the screen. Click once and move the blank image control into the corner.

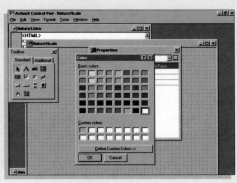

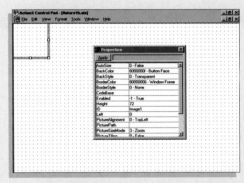

4 Double-click on the Image control and change the properties as follows: PicturePath to C:\CPad12\Nature \backgd04.jpg; PictureSizeMode to 0-Clip; and PictureTiling to 1-True. Close the Properties window, grab the lower right handle on the Image control, drag it to the lower right corner of the screen, and release.

6 When you are done, save the lower .alx file as **Nature1b.alx**. Save the upper half of your page (the old Nature1.alx file) as **Nature1a.alx**. Change the title of your HTML document to **Nature1a.htm** and save your document as **Nature1a.htm**.

5 Now you may begin the task of creative cutting and pasting to resize and reshape your page because you have twice the room.

CHAPTER 13

HTML Templates Demystified

 Templates give you the ability to reuse a good page design over and over again. If you start a Web page from scratch you must have a fresh idea, a design, and then enter all the HTML code and ActiveX controls. A template is created from a document that looks like an existing document. It has color, images, texture, and it can be used again and again. You can create templates from existing Web pages as you come across designs that you like. The CD contains the materials you need for this chapter in the CPad13 folder, which you should copy to your hard drive. For the first part of this chapter we will be using one of the pages from Chapter 12 to demonstrate the use of an HTML Layout control template. The second part of the chapter will involve the creation of a more conventional HTML style area.

How to Use HTML Layout Control Templates

In Chapter 14 we will learn how to create a complete template. For now let's use a template that was created from one of the Web pages in Chapter 12.

 1 With Internet Explorer up and running open the file C:\CPad13\Style1.htm. Although generic the overall "style" of the original document is unchanged.

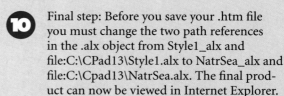

10 Final step: Before you save your .htm file you must change the two path references in the .alx object from Style1_alx and file:C:\CPad13\Style1.alx to NatrSea_alx and file:C:\Cpad13\NatrSea.alx. The final product can now be viewed in Internet Explorer.

9 Change the e-mail address Caption to sbeaches@ savesea.com and click Apply. Remove the remaining borders that were being used for positioning purposes. Due to the fact that the HTML Layout control gives you the versatility to move the controls around you can now make any positioning adjustments you want and the Layout will be ready for scripting with the Script Wizard. Save the Layout as NatrSea.alx.

8 Below the three starfish buttons is a label control that says, "Site Created by xxx.". Change the Caption property to Site Created by Sandy Beaches and click Apply. For the Label control below that double-click on the Picture property. When the Load Picture window appears select Sealogo.gif.

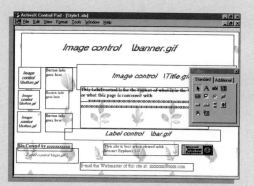

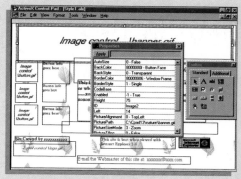

3 All the properties of the various ActiveX controls in this HTML Layout are already set. All you have to do is supply the new file names for the images and text where required. Refer to the picture of the original document to see what changes you should make.

2 Open the same file (C:\CPad13\Style 1.htm) in the ActiveX Control Pad. Click on the .ALX icon in the left margin to open the HTML Layout.

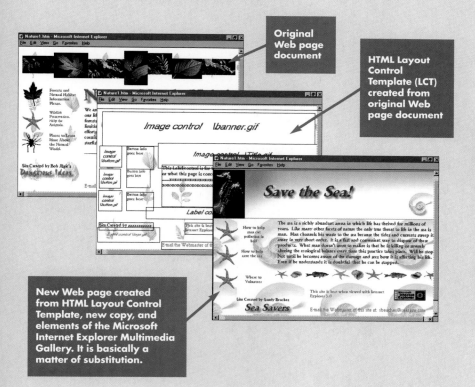

Original Web page document

HTML Layout Control Template (LCT) created from original Web page document

New Web page created from HTML Layout Control Template, new copy, and elements of the Microsoft Internet Explorer Multimedia Gallery. It is basically a matter of substitution.

4 Click once anywhere on the background area to highlight it. Open the Properties window by clicking on the View menu and selecting Properties. Double-click on the PicturePath property and change the path to C:\CPad13\nature\backgd03.jpg. Click Apply. Drag the lower right corner of the new image down and right to the lower right corner of the screen using your mouse, and release.

5 At the top of the page click on the banner graphic area. Change the PicturePath property to C:\CPad13 \nature\banner03.jpg. Using your mouse move the title graphic inside the banner. Change its PicturePath property to C:\CPad13\SaveSea.gif. Click Apply and change the BorderStyle property to 0-None.

7 In this case all three buttons on the left are Image controls and they will have the same PicturePath property, C:\CPad13\nature\images03.gif. Click on the top Image control (button) area and change its PicturePath property. Click Apply. Do the same for the two below. For the Label control to the right of the top starfish replace Button info goes here in the Caption property with How to help man cut pollution in half. Click Apply. For the second starfish Label control change the Caption to How to help save the sea. Click Apply. For the bottom starfish Label control Caption make it Where to volunteer. Click Apply.

6 In the large Label control beneath the banner enter in the Caption property the text from the large graphic that begins: The sea is a richly abundant.... Click Apply. Click on the horizontal bar area next and change the Picture property of that Label control to hruler03.jpg (found in C:\CPad13 \nature\hruler03.jpg). The BackStyle property should be changed to 0-Transparent and the BorderStyle, 0-None.

How to Create Style Areas for HTML Documents

HTML Layout Control Templates (LCT) like the one you just created are for substituting and creating entire Web pages or layouts. Sometimes you are only interested in using a specific area of a Web page. That's why we create style areas. Say, for instance, that you find the Thunderbolt, Inc. Web site, and would like to use their idea of the two lines below the graphic which include a Label control and four OptionButton controls. Here's how to use style areas to incorporate that design into your documents (with Thunderbolt's permission, of course).

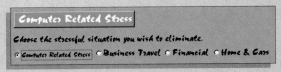

▶ **1** From Internet Explorer open C:\CPad13\abt_thun.htm.

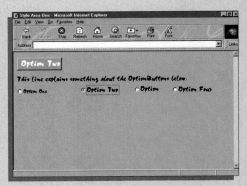

8 Save the file as StyArea1.htm in the CPad13 folder. In Internet Explorer open C:\CPad13\StyArea1.htm. You now have a style area you can use over and over again, anywhere in an HTML document you choose. All you have to do is insert it (cut and paste) into the middle of your existing HTML document, and remove the three sets of tags <HTML>, <TITLE>Style Area One</TITLE>, <BODY>, and </BODY>, and </HTML>.

```
<HTML>
<TITLE>Style Area One</TITLE>
<BODY>
<OBJECT ID="TextBox1" WIDTH=261
 CLASSID="CLSID:8BD21D10-EC42-1
   <PARAM NAME="VariousPropert
```

7 To make sure this a valid HTML document (so you can use it) add the <HTML> tag as the very first line, <TITLE>Style Area One</TITLE> as the second line, and <BODY> as the third line. The last two lines on the page must be </BODY> and </HTML> for the page to work properly.

2 Click on View on the menu bar and select Source.

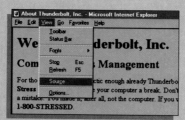

3 When the Windows Notepad opens you will see the code that was used on that page. Using your mouse, highlight the code starting at the first <OBJECT> tag for TextBox1 and ending at the last </OBJECT> tag following OptionButton4. On the menu bar click on Edit and select Copy to put the code onto the Windows Clipboard.

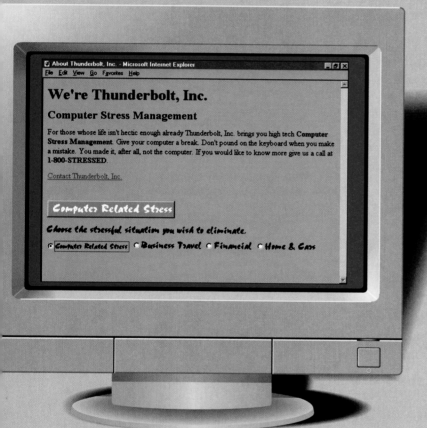

```
<PARAM NAME="VariousPropertyBits" VALUE="746604571">
<PARAM NAME="BackColor" VALUE="8421440">
<PARAM NAME="ForeColor" VALUE="16777215">
<PARAM NAME="Size" VALUE="6900;900">
<PARAM NAME="SpecialEffect" VALUE="1">
<PARAM NAME="FontName" VALUE="Shock">
<PARAM NAME="FontHeight" VALUE="360">
<PARAM NAME="FontCharSet" VALUE="0">
<PARAM NAME="FontPitchAndFamily" VALUE="2">
<PARAM NAME="ParagraphAlign" VALUE="3">
<PARAM NAME="FontWeight" VALUE="0">
</OBJECT>
<BR>
<BR>
<OBJECT ID="Label1" WIDTH=523 HEIGHT=27
CLASSID="CLSID:978C9E23-D4B0-11CE-BF2D-00AA003F40D0">
<PARAM NAME="Caption" VALUE="Choose the stressful situation you wish to e">
<PARAM NAME="Size" VALUE="13806;706">
<PARAM NAME="FontName" VALUE="Shock">
<PARAM NAME="FontHeight" VALUE="320">
<PARAM NAME="FontCharSet" VALUE="0">
<PARAM NAME="FontPitchAndFamily" VALUE="2">
<PARAM NAME="FontWeight" VALUE="0">
</OBJECT>
<BR>
<SCRIPT LANGUAGE="VBScript">
<!--
Sub OptionButton1_Click()
```

4 Click on File on the menu bar and select New. Then click on Edit and select Paste. Make the code in this style section generic so it may be used over and over again. The first object is TextBox1. Nothing has to be changed here. In the second object (Label1) change the Caption Value from "Choose the Stressful situation …" to This line explains something about the OptionButtons below.

5 Move down one step at a time. For Sub OptionButton1_Click() change TextBox1.Text (Computer Related Stress) to read Option One. Likewise in OptionButton1 below that, change the words Computer Related Stress to Option One.

```
</OBJECT>
<BR>
<SCRIPT LANGUAGE="VBScript">
<!--
Sub OptionButton1_Click()
TextBox1.AutoSize = True
TextBox1.BackColor = &H007B7BFF
TextBox1.Text = "Computer Related Stress"
TextBox1.TextAlign = 2
TextBox1.Font.Bold = True
end sub
-->
</SCRIPT>
<OBJECT ID="OptionButton1" WIDTH=179 HEIGHT=29
CLASSID="CLSID:8BD21D50-EC42-11CE-9E0D-00AA006002F3">
<PARAM NAME="VariousPropertyBits" VALUE="1015023643">
<PARAM NAME="BackColor" VALUE="2147483663">
<PARAM NAME="ForeColor" VALUE="2147483666">
<PARAM NAME="DisplayStyle" VALUE="5">
<PARAM NAME="Size" VALUE="4710;767">
<PARAM NAME="Caption" VALUE="Computer Related Stress">
<PARAM NAME="FontName" VALUE="Shock">
<PARAM NAME="FontHeight" VALUE="240">
<PARAM NAME="FontCharSet" VALUE="0">
<PARAM NAME="FontPitchAndFamily" VALUE="2">
<PARAM NAME="FontWeight" VALUE="0">
</OBJECT>
<SCRIPT LANGUAGE="VBScript">
```

6 Repeat this process For OptionButton2. Change Business Travel to Option Two in the two places mentioned above. For OptionButton3 change Financial to Option Three, and for OptionButton4 change Home & Cars to Option Four.

CHAPTER 14

How to Create Templates

 When moving around the Web, you will encounter tons of sites: good, bad, and mediocre. What you should be looking for in general is a site that's straightforward and easy to comprehend. Look for specific elements such as trailers, hypertext graphics, data entry grids, opening paragraphs, bulleted lists, and hypertext type.

In Chapter 13 we learned how to use an HTML layout control template (LCT) and how to construct a style area from part of an existing Web page. In this chapter we will dig a little deeper and actually build an HTML template from scratch that has some of these elements we wish to use. The easiest possible way you can produce a Web page on short notice is to go to a library of generic templates you have created for just such an occasion and simply plug in the words, images, and information that has been provided by the client. Your template library will be built from available samples and the awareness you have developed from viewing thousands of Web sites.

For this chapter it will be assumed that you have begun to grasp a little bit about what HTML code looks like when you come across it. Before you get started copy the CPad14 folder from the CD to your hard drive.

How to Explore HTML Elements for Templates

If you are going to do much in the way of Web site creation in the near future, it won't hurt to become a student of Web page design. As you browse the Web, study the various sites and start to look for clues that could help you in your creative efforts. Notice each element and evaluate how it works (or doesn't work) in that site, and why. There is always a title, and there are always navigational elements like buttons and HTML links, for instance. The next section will show you what to do with these elements once you can recognize them.

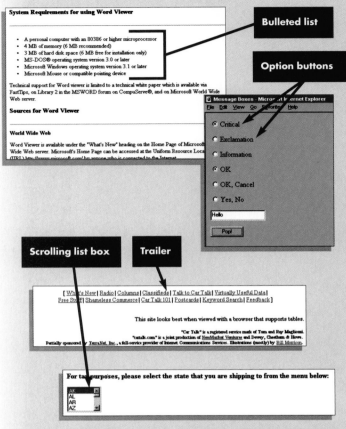

▶ **1** As you're browsing with Internet Explorer and you find a block of type or an element (such as a drop-down list) that you want to use in a Template, you can copy that block. From your Windows Accessories open a blank Windows Notepad.

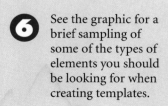

Microsoft Word Viewer version 6.0 for Windows

Microsoft® proudly announces the release of Microsoft Word Viewer, a small application that enables users who do not own Microsoft Word for Windows® to view and print Word documents exactly as they appear in Word. Word Viewer gives users the flexibility to view page layout, zoom, outline, headers/footers, footnotes, and annotations. Word Viewer allows you to read and print Word documents, but it does not allow you to edit them, although you can copy information from the document and activate OLE objects.

Thanks to Word Viewer, people who own any version of Microsoft Word for Windows, or Word for the Macintosh® versions 4.0 and later, can now share their documents with users who do not own Microsoft Word. Compressed, Word Viewer fits onto one 3.5" 1.44 MB floppy disk. We encourage users to copy Word Viewer freely and distribute it to friends and co-workers along with documents they have created in Word format.

Use Word Viewer to view Word documents posted on the Internet

2 Go back to Internet Explorer. Click on View in the Menu bar and then click on Source.

 3 A new windows Notepad will appear with the HTML (or sometimes other scripting) code for the document.

4 Highlight the code by placing the cursor at the start of the text you want. Hold down the mouse button and drag down and to the right as far as you wish to go. Once you have highlighted the text click on the Edit menu and then on Copy.

5 Go back to your Untitled Notepad and click on Edit, then Paste. From the File menu use Save As and name your file (call it **Stycode1.txt**) and store it for a later time. After saving, click on File and New, place the notepad back on the Task bar, and you're ready to get your next piece of code.

6 See the graphic for a brief sampling of some of the types of elements you should be looking for when creating templates.

How to Prepare Code for Templates

Preparing the code for a generic template isn't difficult at all. Based on the code you've copied in the previous pages, you'll break that original code into areas and replace existing wording with generic terms that you can later easily remove or replace.

▶ **1** In Internet Explorer, go to the Web site you wish to use as a basis for your template, such as the simple page you see in the graphic (Danger1.htm in the CPad14\Danger). Click View on the Menu bar, then Source to see the code.

Welcome to the name of the site. This is where the opening explanation goes and it should just fill up an much of the area as needed. Welcome to the name of the site. This is where the opening explanation goes and it should just fill up an much of the area as needed. Welcome to the name of the site. This is where the opening explanation goes and it should just fill up an much of the area as needed.

8 Open your Internet Explorer and open the C:\CPad14\ WebTemp1.htm file. What you see is a generic representation of the Web page you started with. You have now created a Template you can use over and over.

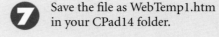

7 Save the file as WebTemp1.htm in your CPad14 folder.

2 Now you'll redo the code so that it's more generic, and therefore easier to reuse. Divide the code into several sections by inserting blank lines between them, as shown in the large graphic. This program was divided into four sections, but that number will be different for each template you create, based on the design.

```
<HTML>
<HEAD>
<TITLE>Web Template One</TITLE>
</HEAD>
<BODY BGCOLOR=WHITE>
<CENTER>
<IMG SRC="Image1.jpg" HEIGHT=60 WIDTH=100>
<IMG SRC="Title Image.gif">
<IMG SRC="Image2.jpg" HEIGHT=60 WIDTH=100>
<BR><BR>
<IMG SRC="Anybar.gif">
<BR><BR>
```

3 In the first section change the title to Web Template One, the images to Image1.jpg, TitleImage.gif, and Image2.jpg. Make the bar read Anybar.gif. These are the generic placeholder names that you'll replace with your own information each time you use this template to create a Web page.

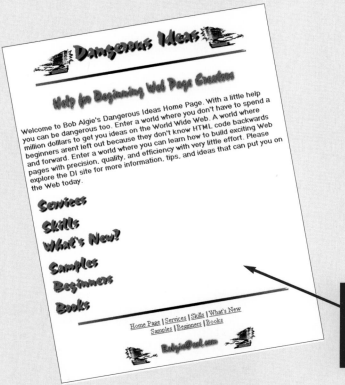

Divide the code into easily understood sections before converting into generic terms.

```
<IMG SRC="Headline or Headline Graphic" HEIGHT=88 WIDTH=468>
<BR></CENTER>
<FONT COLOR=BLUE FACE="MS Sans Serif" SIZE=3>
<B>Welcome to the name of the site. This is where  the opening
explanation goes and it should just fill up an much of the area
as needed.Welcome to the name of the site. This is where  the opening
explanation goes and it should just fill up an much of the area
as needed.Welcome to the name of the site. This is where  the opening
explanation goes and it should just fill up an much of the area
as needed.
</B></FONT>
```

4 In the second section change the Helpfor.gif to Headline or Headline Graphic. Replace the body copy with anything you like just to portray the style. The words don't have to mean anything right now.

```
<BR><BR>
<A HREF="Site_1.htm"><IMG SRC="Site_1.gif" BORDER=NO></A><BR>
<A HREF="Site_2.htm"><IMG SRC="Site_2.gif" BORDER=NO></A><BR>
<A HREF="Site_3.htm"><IMG SRC="Site_3.gif" BORDER=NO></A><BR>
<A HREF="Site_4.htm"><IMG SRC="Site_4.gif" BORDER=NO></A><BR>
<A HREF="Site_5.htm"><IMG SRC="Site_5.gif" BORDER=NO></A><BR>
<A HREF="Site_6.htm"><IMG SRC="Site_6.gif" BORDER=NO></A><BR>
<BR>
<P>
<CENTER>
<IMG SRC="Bar2.gif">
<BR><BR>
```

5 The third section is a list of hypertext graphics. When you click on them they will take you to another site. Change these as you see here. Change the Bar2.gif to Anybar.gif.

```
<!-- TRAILER BEGINS -->
<P>
<CENTER>
<A HREF="/">Home Page</A> | <A HREF="/Site_1.htm/">Site 1</A> |
<A HREF="/Site_2.htm/">Site 2</A> | <A HREF="/Site_3.htm/">Site 3</A><BR>
<A HREF="/Site_4.htm">Site 4</A> | <A HREF="/Site_5.htm/">Site 5</A> |
<A HREF="/Site_6.htm/">Site 6</A><P>
<!--TRAILER ENDS -->
</CENTER>
<IMG SRC="Image.jpg" HEIGHT=50 WIDTH=75>
<IMG SRC="Logoimage.gif" HEIGHT=50 WIDTH=160>
<IMG SRC="Image.jpg" HEIGHT=50 WIDTH=75>
</CENTER>
<BR><BR>
</BODY>
</HTML>
```

6 In the footer leave Home Page but change services to Site_1, skills to Site_2 and so on. Make the image names more generic, too.

TRY IT!

Now you will get the opportunity to create a couple of style sheets based on an existing site, and then use the concept to create new pages of your own.

Style sheets can be especially helpful if you need to create a Web page on short notice. If you begin to squirrel away a library of these now, in the future you can quickly create a prototype page when someone needs it *right now*, then embellish the page and add more controls after the initial design is approved.

The files for this exercise are provided in the CPTry4 folder on the CD.

Open the Thunder2.htm file in Internet Explorer and click on the HotSpots or hypertext to see how the site performs. Is this what you want to use to create a style sheet? (YES!) Try it!

```
<HTML>
<HEAD>
<TITLE>WebStyle1.htm</TITLE>
</HEAD>
<BODY BGCOLOR=white>
```

With the Thunder2.htm file open in the ActiveX Control Pad, change the title from We're Thunderbolt, Inc. to WebStyle1.htm. Change the BGCOLOR (background color) from yellow to WHITE to make your style sheet a little more basic in nature.

```
<CENTER>
<H1>Company Name goes here</H1>
<A HREF="contact.htm"><IMG SRC="Logo here.xxx" HEIGHT=75 WIDTH=75></A>
<H2>Topic or Subhead here</H2>
</CENTER>
```

Change the <H1> heading to Company Name goes here. Change the <A HREF... link from Contact.htm to WebStyle2.htm. You will create this style sheet in just a few minutes. For the <IMG SRC=... change it to read Logo here.xxx, and for the <H2> change it to Topic or subhead here.

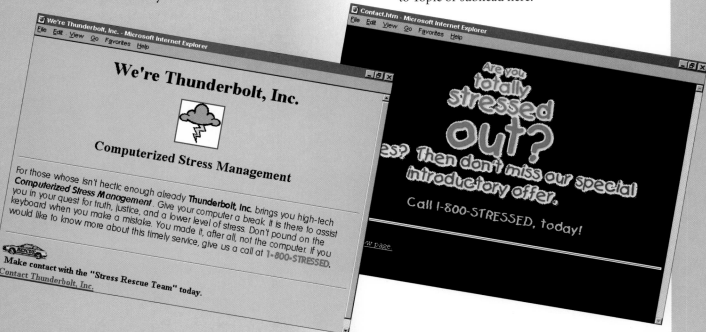

```
<P>
<FONT FACE="Elementary SF" SIZE=3>This is where the copy goes that begins the
description of the matter mentioned in the sub-heading.  <B>Insert bold type or company
name where needed.</B> brings you high-tech<B></I> this is bold & italic for further
emphasis </I></B>. More generic copy goes here for the style sheet. Descriptive stuff
concerning the topic is in here. Start to wrap it up here so you don't exceed the limits
of your style sheet. If you would like to know more about this timely service, give us
a call at <B><FONT COLOR=RED>1-800-red and bold for emphasis</FONT></B>.
</P>
```

Change the
<P> paragraph to the block of
"placeholder" text shown here.

```
<P>
<HR>
<IMG SRC="optional image.xxx" Height=25 WIDTH=80>
<MARQUEE  DIRECTION=LEFT BEHAVIOR=SLIDE SCROLLAMOUNT=10
SCROLLDELAY=100>Optional sliding marquee copy goes here. </MARQUEE>
```

The image and the marquee are optional.
Change the image SRC from "car.gif" to
"Optional Image.xxx." Change the sliding
copy on the marquee to Optional sliding
marque copy goes here.

```
<A HREF="WebStyle2.htm"><B>Contact Company Name</B></A>
</BODY>
</HTML>
```

The hypertext <A HREF=… is not optional because it gets you to the second
page. Change "Contact.htm" to
"WebStyle2.htm" and change
Thunderbolt, Inc. to Company Name.

7

From the File menu choose Save As,
and save this page to your CPTry4
folder with the name WebStyle1.htm.
Be sure to us the Save As option and
change the file name from
Thunder2.htm to WebStyle1.htm or
your original file will be overwritten.

```
<HTML>
<HEAD>
<TITLE>Contact.htm</TITLE>
</HEAD>
<BODY BGCOLOR=BLACK>
<CENTER>
<IMG SRC="Stress1.gif">
<P>
<H2><FONT COLOR=YELLOW FACE="Kidz">Call 1-800-STRESSED,  today!</FONT></H2>
</CENTER>
<HR COLOR=BLUE SIZE=5>
<BR>
<A HREF="Thunder2.htm">Return to yellow page.</A>
</BODY>
</HTML>
```

While still in
the ActiveX
Control Pad,
open contact.htm. As you see there is
very little code involved.

```
<HTML>
<HEAD>
<TITLE>WebStyle2.htm</TITLE>
</HEAD>
<BODY BGCOLOR=WHITE>
```

Change the
title from Contact.htm to WebStyle2.htm, and
the background color to BGCOLOR=WHITE.

```
<CENTER>
<IMG SRC="Big Image.xxx" HEIGHT=200 WIDTH=400>
```

Change *<IMG SRC="Stress1.gif ">* to **<IMG
SRC="BigImage.xxx" HEIGHT=200
WIDTH=400>**. The *height* and *width* attributes
leave space on our style sheet for the graphic.

11

```
<P>
<H2><FONT COLOR=BLACK FACE="MS Sans Serif" >Call 1-800-XXX-XXXX,
today!</FONT></H2>
</CENTER>
```

For Heading 2 <H2> change the FONT
COLOR= to BLACK, and the FACE= to
"MS Sans Serif" because you don't know
what type face you will be using in the fu-
ture. In the phone number change the word
STRESSED to XXX-XXXX.

12

```
<HR COLOR=BLACK SIZE=5>
<BR>
<A HREF="WebStyle1.htm">Return to the previous page.</A>
</BODY>
</HTML>
```

Change the
color of the horizontal rule <HR> to BLACK.
Change the link to <A HREF="WebStyle1
.htm">Return to the previous page</A>.

Use the Save
As option to
save this doc-
ument in
your CPTry4
folder as
WebStyle2
.htm. Open
or restore Internet Explorer. Then open
WebStyle1.htm and view what your completed style sheet looks like. Click the link
to see how it works.

Continue to next page ▶

TRY IT!

Continue
below

It is fortunate that you just created this style sheet because ACME/GEN-ERAL Mining & Landscape, Inc. just called. They want you to get them on the Web *right now!* "Nothing elaborate," they tell you. "Just a couple of pages with a phone number." And you, being the forward-thinker that you are, have the situation under complete control.

14

```
<HTML>
<HEAD>
<TITLE>ACME/GENERAL Web site</TITLE>
</HEAD>
```

In the ActiveX Control Pad, open your WebStyle1.htm file and change the title to ACME/GENERAL Web site.

15

```
<BODY BGCOLOR=white>
<CENTER>
<H1>ACME/GENERAL mining & landscaping</H1>
```

Make the main heading ACME/GEN-ERAL mining & landscaping.

16

```
<A HREF="ACME2.htm"><IMG SRC="aglogo2.gif" HEIGHT=80 WIDTH=110></A>
<H2>If it can be dug, we'll dig it!</H2>
</CENTER>
<HR>
```

For the image link fill in <A HREF="ACME2.htm"><IMG SRC="aglogo2.gif" HEIGHT=80 WIDTH=110</A>. The height and width of this image link will vary based on the dimensions of the image you are using. This is the hypertext logo that will take you to the other page. For the <H2> sub heading fill in If it can be dug, we'll dig it!

17

Type in the copy as it is shown here.

```
<P>
<FONT FACE="Elementary SF" SIZE=3>Every mining company in the world would like to
say, <B>"We've struck it rich!"</B> In a way, we have. <B><I> ACME/GENERAL </I></B>
has given up digging for burried treasure, but we still like to move lots of dirt and rock.
Why not? We're good at it. We like to plant things too and watch them grow. This is why
we have given up mining (but not our name) and have become the best landscape
architects, soil remediators, and conservation consultants in the business today. Just
growing list of satisfied customers. If you would like to know more about our amazing
company give us a call at <B><FONT COLOR=RED>1-800-DigDEEP</FONT></FONT></B>.
</P>
<HR>
```

```
<IMG SRC="blutruk.gif" Height=50 WIDTH=80>
<MARQUEE DIRECTION=LEFT BEHAVIOR=SLIDE SCROLLAMOUNT=10
SCROLLDELAY=100>Free estimates are always available.</MARQUEE>
```

ACME wants to keep the small image and the sliding marquee at the bottom of the page, so change the image line to <IMG SRC="blutruk.gif" HEIGHT=50 WIDTH=80>, and the marquee copy to Free estimates are always available.

```
<A HREF="ACME2.htm"><B>ACME/GENERAL mining & landscaping, inc.</B></A>
</BODY>
</HTML>
```

To enable your users to navigate to the second page, you need to change the hypertext line to <A HREF="ACME2.htm"> <B>ACME/GENERAL mining & landscape, inc.</B></A>.

Use Save As to save the document as ACME1.htm in your CPTry4 folder. Open up WebStyle2.htm in the ActiveX Control Pad.

```
<HTML>
<HEAD>
<TITLE>ACME2.htm</TITLE>
</HEAD>
<BODY BGCOLOR=WHITE>
<CENTER>
<IMG SRC="aglogo.gif">
```

Change the title to ACME2.htm and the image to <IMG SRC="aglogo.gif">. You can delete the height and width attributes because you no longer need to reserve that space.

```
<P>
<H2><FONT COLOR=BLACK FACE="MS Sans Serif">Call 1-800-DigDEEP,
today!</FONT></H2>
</CENTER>
<HR COLOR=BLACK SIZE=5>
<BR>
<A HREF="ACME1.htm">Return to the previous page.</A>
</BODY>
</HTML>
```

The only line of copy on this page is for the phone number. Change it to Call 1-800-DigDEEP. And finally change the hypertext link to <A HREF="ACME1.htm">Return to the previous page.</A>.

From the File menu use Save As to save ACME2.htm, then Restore Internet Explorer and view your work. Because you had a style sheet you are ready to deliver to Acme/ General in a very short time span.

CHAPTER 15

How to Use the TabStrip Control

The ActiveX Control Pad comes with the TabStrip control, which allows you to display a lot of categorized information, like a group of files in a filing cabinet. The TabStrip control can be created easily in the HTML Layout Control. Coding it properly can be more involved than some other controls we've seen, but you'll be able to do it easily by now. To insert a TabStrip control you'll use both the left and right mouse buttons, so click carefully.

A TabStrip control looks like a stack of file folders. All the folders contain information on the same subject matter, and each tabbed folder in the control is structured like the others. However, each tab contains specific information.

To see a TabStrip control use Internet Explorer to open the *TScar.htm* file from the CPad15 folder on the CD (which you should copy to your hard drive before beginning this chapter).

Follow along carefully and you will be able to create a simple TabStrip control, linking the tabs together with the .alx file.

How to Make a TabStrip Control

In this exercise, we'll make a TabStrip control in which each page contains three labels: one for the name of the vehicle, a little larger one for information about the vehicle, and a third label with a tag line. When you get to the coding part in the next spread don't be too concerned. Just follow directions carefully and you will have a working TabStrip control that you can use as a template for other TabStrip controls.

```
<HTML>
<HEAD>
<TITLE>TabCars.htm</TITLE>
</HEAD>
<BODY>
<CENTER>
<H1>What type of car are you looking for?</H1>
Click on the tab with your choice of vehicle.

</CENTER>
</BODY>
</HTML>
```

1 From your ActiveX Control Pad open a new HTML Text Editor screen. Put TabCars2.htm in the title block. In the BODY area type <CENTER> and on the next line type the header <H1>**What type of car are you looking for?**</H1>. Below that type **Click on a tab with your choice of vehicle,** skip a line and close the centered block with </CENTER>.

▶ **By using the Style property you can set your TabStrip control to have tabs or buttons, and TabOrientation lets you put the tabs on the right, left, top, or bottom.**

▶ **The TabStrip is a very useful and space-saving item. By using the MultiRow property you can literally have a page full of tabs. For instance, an alphabetical or individual listing of employees in a specific department could be "filed" in one TabStrip control.**

▶ **Once you open a Properties window in the HTML Layout control, leave it open while you are working there. The properties of whatever control you are working on will be displayed as you move from control to control.**

8 Adjust the properties for your Label controls as follows: For all three labels set the BackColor property to the same gray as the TabStrip control. Set the Caption for Label3 to **Choose Your Car Here,** and the FONT property to MS Sans Serif, Bold, Italic, Size 18. Change the ForeColor to bright blue. Set TextAlign to 2-Center. For Label2 set the FONT properties to MS Sans Serif, Bold, Italic, Size 14. Make the ForeColor property the same as the background of the Layout, delete the Caption, change SpecialEffect to 2-Sunken, and TextAlign to 2-Center. For Label1 set the Caption to read **Click on a tab to choose a car.** Set the Font properties to MS Sans Serif, Size 12, and SpecialEffect to 2-Sunken. For the properties on the TabStrip control set the BackColor to the same color as the background of the Layout. Set the TabFixedWidth property to 55, the FONT to MS Sans Serif, Bold, Size 10, and the ForeColor property to red.

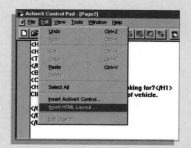

2 Place the cursor on the blank line you left in the body of the code and left-click once. From the Edit menu select Insert HTML Layout. Name the new file TabCars2.alx and save it in the CPad15 folder.

3 Click on the .ALX icon in the left margin to open the HTML Layout.

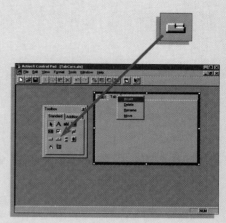

4 From the toolbox click on the TabStrip control icon. A new control with two tabs will appear. Place the cursor on Tab2 and right-click once. In the small menu box left-click on Insert and a new tab will appear. Repeat this for a fourth tab.

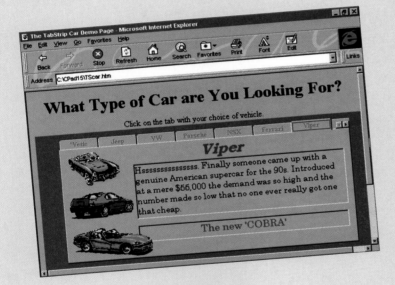

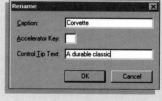

6 Caption the remaining tabs as **NSX** for Tab2, **CIVIC** for Tab3, and **Indy Car** for Tab4. For Control Tip Text in Tab2 put **A technological marvel,** Tab3 **Practicality personified,** and Tab4 **Faster than a speeding bullet.**

5 You can rename the tabs the same way you added more tabs. Move the cursor to Tab1 and right-click, then left-click on Rename to open a small dialog box. Type **Corvette** for the Caption and **A durable classic** in the Control Tip Text area. Control tips are the words in the little boxes that pop up when the cursor is placed on the tab. Click OK.

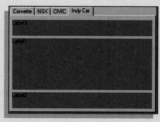

7 From the toolbox place Label1 in the middle of the TabStrip control, then Label2 at the bottom and Label3 just under the tabs.

How to Script the TabStrip Control

You have diligently set up your TabStrip control and now it is time to add the magic. What you are going to do involves scripting with VBScript. *Type the code exactly as it is presented and don't worry about why or how it works.* Most of the code is generated by the HTML Layout Control and the Script Wizard. You only have to type in a few lines. When completed you will have a perfectly working TabStrip control.

▶ **1** In the Control Pad, open your TabCars2.htm from the previous page, and click the Script Wizard icon.

6 Save the TabCars2.alx file for the last time. Restore Internet Explorer and open the TabCars2.htm file. When you give it a try you should have a working TabStrip control.

2 In the Event pane (left) of the Script Wizard locate TabStrip1 and click on the plus (+). Below that select the Click event. Drop down the very bottom where you see the option buttons for Code View and List View. Click on the Code View option button. This opens a little VBScript editor and supplies the first line of code for you. After this first line, add these four lines exactly as shown:

Label1.Caption=Picture(Index)

Label3.Caption=TabStrip1.Tabs(Index).Caption

Label2.Caption=CarWords(Index) end sub

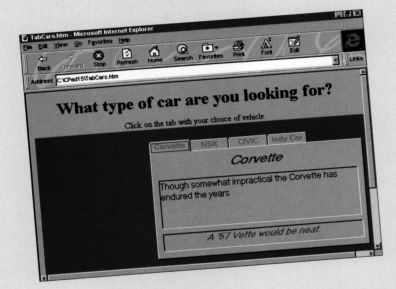

3 When you click the option back to List View you will notice the following message in pane #3.

4 It is very important to save this file now! When you save your TabCars2.htm file at this point you are ensuring that the four lines of script you just created will be written automatically into the TabCars2.alx file where you can modify or add to it.

5 From Windows 95 Accessories open a Windows Notepad. Open your TabCars2.alx file. What you see is all the code generated by the HTML Layout Control and the Script Wizard. Immediately after the lines that begin with <SCRIPT LANGUAGE="VBSCRIPT> and <!—, carefully fill in all the lines exactly as shown, until you reach the line that reads Sub TabStrip1_Click(ByVal Index). Be careful. Anything you miss or type in wrong will cause an error when you try to run the TabCars2.htm in Internet Explorer.

CHAPTER 16

HTML Tables

 The most popular format for organizing and visualizing data is the use of tables. Tables are a way of providing large amounts of visual information in an organized manner. As you will learn in this chapter, they can be used to display a wide variety of items. They are useful for lining up material vertically and horizontally, making creative layouts, and placing text beside graphics.

The second part of this chapter will demonstrate the enhanced table feature of ActiveX.

The example for this chapter can be found in the CPad16 folder on the CD.

How to Create a Table

A table is a very useful and versatile tool. Here you will learn how to build a simple table and find out a few of the things you can do with it.

▶ **1** Open the ActiveX Control Pad. In the body area type in <TABLE BORDER> which will place a thin border around all the table cells.

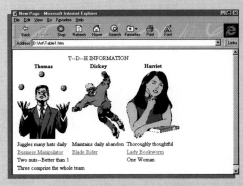

9 If you start out with <TABLE> instead of <TABLE BORDER> your table will be borderless.

8 Save the table as Table1.htm in your CPad16 folder. Open and view the completed table in Internet Explorer (refer to main graphic).

2 Type <CAPTION>
T—D-H INFORMATION
</CAPTION> to place
a caption on top of
your table.

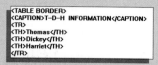

```
<TABLE BORDER>
<CAPTION>T–D–H INFORMATION</CAPTION>
<TR>
<TH>Thomas</TH>
<TH>Dickey</TH>
<TH>Harriet</TH>
</TR>
```

3 Tables are built row by row starting with <TR> and ending with the </TR> tag. Type <TR> to start your first
table row. Use <TH>…</TH> for table headings and type
<TH>Thomas</TH><TH>Dickey</TH><TH>Harriet
</TH>. End the row by typing </TR>.

4 The next row will hold the images of our
three people. Type <TR> and then
<TD><IMG SRC="juggler.jpg
HEIGHT=200 WIDTH=150"></TD>
<TD><IMG SRC="blader.jpg"
HEIGHT=200 WIDTH=150></TD>
<TD><IMG SRC="thought.jpg"
HEIGHT=200 WIDTH=150></TD> and
end with </TR> (Note that image height
and width are set in pixels).

```
<TR>
<TD><IMG SRC="juggler.jpg" HEIGHT=200 WIDTH=150></TD>
<TD><IMG SRC="blader.jpg" HEIGHT=200 WIDTH=150></TD>
<TD><IMG SRC="thought.jpg" HEIGHT=200 WIDTH=150></TD>
</TR>
<TR>
<TD>Juggles many hats daily</TD>
<TD>Maintains daily abandon</TD>
<TD>Thoroughly thoughtful     </TD>
</TR>
```

5 The next row will contain descrip-
tive data. Type <TR>
<TD>Juggles many hats</TD>
<TD>Maintains daily aban-
don</TD><TD>Thoroughly
thoughtful</TD></TR>.

```
<TR>
<TD COLSPAN=2>Two nuts–Better than 1</TD>
<TD>One Woman</TD>
</TR>
<TR>
<TD COLSPAN=3>Three comprise the whole team</TD>
</TR>
</TABLE>
```

```
<TR>
<TD><A HREF=http://www.busyjuggler.com>Business Manipulator</A>
<TD><A HREF=http://www.blademan.com>Blade Rider</A>
<TD><A HREF=http://www.bookworm.com>Lady Bookworm</A>
</TR>
```

7 To demonstrate the spanning of columns or rows
place the following beneath the first four rows you
have already created. Type <TR><TD
COLSPAN=2>Two nuts—Better than one</TD>
<TD>OneWoman</TD></TR><TR><TD
COLSPAN=3>Three comprise the whole
team</TR>. End with </TABLE> to close the table.

6 Hyperlinks to each of the three sites will be in the
next row. Type <TR><TD>
<A HREF=http://www.busyjuggler.com>
Business Manipulator></A></TD><TD>
<A HREF=http://www.blademan.com>Blade
Rider></A></TD> <TD>
<A HREF=http://www.bookworm.com>Lady
Bookworm</A></TD> (/TR>.

How to Use the Enhanced Tables Feature

Tables can do a lot more than show columns of data on a gray background—you can now use them as a design element on your pages. Enhanced tables allow you to introduce a background other than just the plain old neutral gray, like the table you created earlier in this chapter.

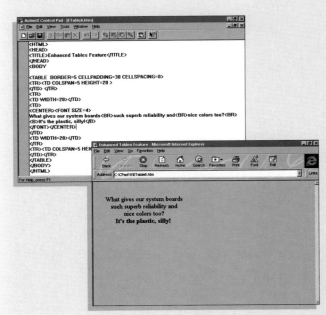

 1 In your Internet Explorer open the Etable6.htm file. Although this is a table, it isn't displayed properly. It just looks like type. Open the same file in the ActiveX Control Pad to view the code.

 7 Adding the background and color one more time near the end will finish the table and fill the cells all around the center.

TIP SHEET

▶ In the beginning tag, if you change **<TABLE RULES=NONE>** to **<TABLE RULES=COLS>** you will get your rules between the columns. **RULES=ROWS** will give you rules between the rows.

▶ A very similar looking graphic can be produced without writing code with the HTML Layout Control (but your result won't be a table). For the base area use a CommandButton with the enabled property set to false. The green board can be the first of two image controls and the red board the last. Then add the type in a Label control with the BackStyle set to Transparent and the font increased to size 10, and its ForeColor set to light yellow. You'll get the same visible result, but from a different approach.

```
<HTML>
<HEAD>
<TITLE>Enhanced Tables Feature</TITLE>
</HEAD>
<BODY>
<TABLE RULES=NONE>
<TABLE  BORDER=5 CELLPADDING=30 CELLSPACING=0>
```

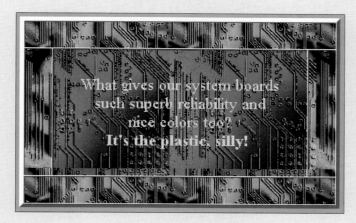

2 Just after the <BODY> tag add the line <TABLE RULES=NONE>. This will give you a table with an outside border but no rules around each table cell.

```
<TD>
<CENTER><FONT COLOR=#ffffcc SIZE=4>
What gives our system boards<BR>such su
<B>It's the plastic, silly!</B>
</FONT></CENTER>
</TD>
```

3 You can add some color to the font by changing the Font line just before the copy. Add COLOR= #ffffcc as seen in the graphic.

```
<BODY
<TABLE RULES=NONE>
<TABLE  BORDER=5 CELLPADDING=30 CELLSPACING=0>
<TR><TD COLSPAN=5 HEIGHT=20 BACKGROUND="grenbord.gif" BGCOLOR=#E8CCA0>
```

4 It is really simple to add a background graphic and background color to a cell. After HEIGHT=20, type in **BACKGROUND= "grenbord.gif" BGCOLOR= #E8CCA0** on the third line of the body. This fills the top cell of the table. Be sure the > sign comes after your addition, not after HEIGHT=20.

```
<TR>
<TD WIDTH=20 BACKGROUND="grenbord.gif" BGCOLOR=#E8CCA0></TD>
<TD>
<CENTER><FONT COLOR=#ffffcc SIZE=4>
What gives our system boards<BR>such superb reliability and<BR>nice colors too?<BR>
<B>It's the plastic, silly!</B>
</FONT></CENTER>
</TD>
<TD WIDTH=20 BACKGROUND="grenbord.gif" BGCOLOR=#E8CCA0></TD>
</TR>
```

6 Typing in **BACKGROUND="grenbord.gif" BGCOLOR=#8ECCA0** on either side of the copy for the visible words fills the two side cells. Follow the graphic carefully to add this information.

```
<BODY
<TABLE RULES=NONE>
<TABLE  BORDER=5 CELLPADDING=30 CELLSPACING=0
BACKGROUND="redbord.gif" BGCOLOR=#572b00>
```

5 Adding the line BACKGROUND="redbord.gif" BGCOLOR=#572b00> on the line that begins with <TABLE BORDER=5... initiates a red background in the entire table. Be sure to re-moved the > from the previous line.

TRY IT!

Let's put your expertise to work. You are now going to create a complete Web site. Assume that all the correct planning has been done in advance, and that you have gathered all of the graphics, links, and basic information that you need. Before you begin, copy the CPTry5 folder to your hard drive. You have the knowledge to create a great site, so let's get going.

World Wide Wolf Home Page - Microsoft Internet Explorer

File Edit View Go Favorites Help

WELCOME TO THE WORLD WIDE WOLF
A SHORT INTRODUCTION

This page viewed best with

The wolf is perhaps the most misunderstood animal on the face of the earth today. Because of man's inability to live in the proximity of wild animals combined with folklore, myths, legends, politics, and fairy tales, the wolf has been hunted, tortued, and nearly driven to extinction. Wolves are a wonderful natural treasure and it is encouraging to see the wide and varied sites that are available for you to view on the Web. (See Wolf Links) Following are some interesting facts about wolves, their lives, and their nature.
There is no documented account of a healthy wolf ever attacking a human. It is very likely that at one time or another the land your home is on was once the home of a wolf pack (greatest natural range of any mammal except humans). Pups are born completely blind and deaf, depending on their mother and other members of the pack. The whole pack takes care of and raises the pups (non-breeding females produce milk and males compete to baby sit). Each pack has a leading, dominant pair (male and female) called the Alpha. Dominant males can staredown other wolves in the pack to prevent a fight and dominant females do the same to prevent other females from mating with her mate (fights are very rare). Some members stay with the pack for life. Wolves can run up to 40 miles per hour and can easily cover 50 mile a day. By smell alone wolves can locate prey, other pack members or enemies. It can tell them if other wolves were in their territory, if they were male or female, and how recently they visited. Less than one percent of sheep and cattle are killed each year by wolves. Loss of cattle to poisonous plants, disease, and poor husbandry account for far more livestock deaths. Wolves howl to communicate, advertise their existence, warn off intruders, greet other wolves, mark their territory, gather the pack, or just for pure enjoyment. Wolves never howl at the full moon (but call the pack together because visibility is good for hunting). Wolves also communicate by the position of the tail, lips, nose, and ears.

WOLF LINKS
LINKS TO OTHER WOLF PAGES AND SOURCES OF INFORMATION.

Click on the picture of the wolf to transfer to the Wolf Links Page.

THIS SITE WAS CREATED BY Bob Algie's Dangerous Ideas

Contact the Site Author:
ralgie@aol.com

Credits: Most of the information about wolves on this page is borrowed from Steven Today's wolf page, "Howling Mad!" The wolf pictures are from the Authour's collection of clip art except for the two larger ones which are from the Minnesota Wolf Project - 1994. Titles, bars, backgrounds, and other art was created by Bob Algie's Dangerous Ideas specifically for this project. They were created completely from scratch using Paint Shop Pre beta version 4.12 . Any resemblence to

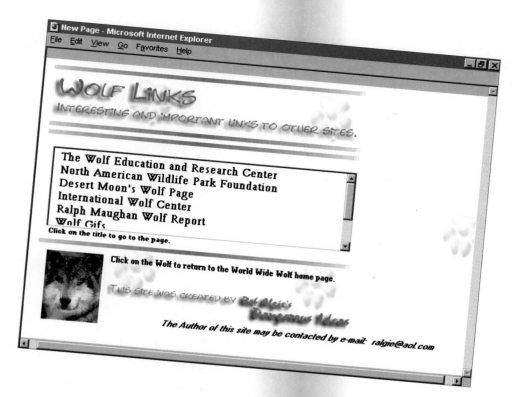

Open your
Internet
Explorer and
your ActiveX
Control Pad
with a blank
HTML Text

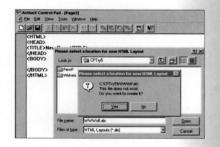

Editor. In the body open an HTML Layout
control (Edit, Insert HTML Layout). Make
sure you are creating your .alx file in the
CPTry5 folder; name the file WWWolfa.alx.

Click on the .ALX (HTML Layout) icon
in the left margin to open the layout.
Start with the background. From the
HTML Layout toolbox click on the
Image control icon and place the control
in the upper left corner of the layout.

Open the
Properties
window for
the Image
control by
clicking on
the View menu and Properties. Double-
click on the PicturePath property and
type in **C:\CPTry5\printbak.gif.**

Change the PictureSizeMode to
0-Clip with a double-click, and
PictureTiling to -1-True. Grab the
handle at the lower right corner
of the image, hold down the left
mouse key, drag it to the lower right
corner of the Layout and release.

Continue to next page ▶

TRY IT!

Continue below

6

Reopen the first (WWWolfa.alx) of your three Layout controls. From the toolbox, center a large Label control near the top of the page. Change the BackStyle property to 0-Transparent, delete the Caption and double-click on the Picture property. Locate the file named WWW1.gif in the CPTry5 folder, click on the name and the Open.

7

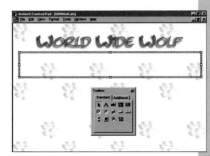

Select an Image control from the toolbox and draw it out nearly the width of the screen under the title.

8

Change the property of the Picture-Path to C:\CPTtry5 \bigbar.gif. Adjust the box to fit nearly across the page by moving the handles. Place six similarly shaped Label controls in this box.

9

On each of the six labels change the BackStyle property to 0-Transparent, delete the Caption, and consecutively change the Picture properties to W1.gif, W2.gif, W3.gif, W4.gif, W5.gif, and W6.gif.

5

Save the Layout and close the file. You are going to need a longer page which can be made with two more HTML Layouts below the first one you created. Create two more HTML Layouts and name them WWWolf2a.alx and WWWolf3a .alx. Add the background graphics to them, as you did in steps 2-4. Save and close them.

10

After you adjust the pictures (Labels) so they look right, there will be extra room. Keep introducing similar Label controls until they fill the bar across the page. Set their properties the same as the others. There are a total of nine pictures available for you in the CPTry5 folder.

11

Insert an Image control below the row of pictures to house a horizontal bar. Double-click on the PicturePath property and enter C:\CPTry5\bar10.gif. Place another Image control at the left side of the bar and change its PicturePath to C:\CPTry5\pawbutn.gif. Place the button over the left end of the bar.

12

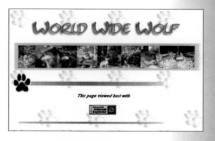

Centered below the bar place a Label control with the properties set to BackStyle (0-Transparent), Caption (This page viewed best with), Font (MS Serif, Bold Italic, Size 10), and TextAlign (2-Center). Place another Label below that one and set it's properties to BackStyle (0-Transparent), delete the Caption, and select ielogo.gif for the Picture property. Place a HotSpot control inside the logo itself. Change its Mouse Pointer property to 2-Cross. This is going to house a hypertext function. Place one more Image control (for another horizontal bar) below and set its PicturePath property to C:\CPTry5\bar5.gif.

13

Save this layout, close it, and open the Layout for the middle section of the page (WWWolf2a.alx) with a click on the center .ALX icon.

14

Place an Image control across the top of the Layout to house a title. Set the PicturePath to C:\CPTry5\Welcome.gif. Place an Image control on the left and make it about 2 inches square. Set the PicturePath to C:\CPTry5\Wface2.gif and AutoSize to -1-True.

15

To the right of the Image place a Label control. Back-Style should be set to 0-Trans-parent, Font (MS Serif, Bold, Size 10). For the Caption double-click and enter the words as shown in the large graphic on these pages (or copy them from the CD). When you reach the bottom of the picture of the wolf, create another label across the entire page with the same properties. Copy in all the text. (When typing you can hit the Enter key every once in a while to see how your Label is filling up. Hit the "End" key to return to your place on the line you were typing.)

16

At the beginning we will place a Label control containing a tiny "paw button." To do this, create one Label control and select the pawbutn.gif you used before. BackStyle property is 0-Transparent and the Caption is deleted. Once you have your small Image click on the Edit menu and select Copy. This puts it on the clipboard and all you need to do is to click on Edit, and Paste each time you need another one. Add these buttons to the rest of the text where they belong.

Continue to next page ▶

TRY IT!

Continue
below

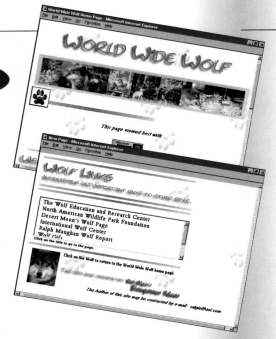

 17

When you reach the bottom of the
Layout save it and close. Click on the
third .ALX icon (WWWolf3a.alx) to
open the Layout and continue.

18

If you are not done with the copy block,
create another Label and complete the
copy. Place an Image control under your
type for a horizontal bar and change the
PicturePath property to C:\CPTry5
\bar5.gif. Place another Image across the
page for a title and set its PicturePath
property to C:\CPTry5\Links.gif.

 19

Just below the
title place two
Labels. For
the first (left
Label) set
BackStyle to
0-Transpar-
ent, delete the
Caption and locate wface1.gif for
the Picture. For the other Label set the
BackStyle to 0-Transparent and the
Caption to Click on the picture of the
Wolf to transfer to the Wolf Links Page.
Change the Font to MS Serif, Bold Italic.

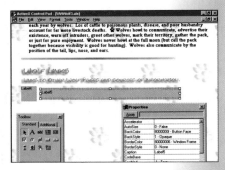

 20

Copy and Paste another bar like the first
and place it under the wolf picture. Place
a HotSpot control inside the picture leaving a margin around it for access to the
Label if we need to modify it.

 21

Below the bar create another Image control for a title and change the Picture-
Path property to C:\CPTry5\created.gif.

 22

Add any Labels controls you need to
include contact information, credits,
or copyrights. Save the Layout, close it,
and save the entire HTML document.

 23

Open the page (WWWolfa.htm) in
Internet Explorer to view the raw document you have created. It should look
similar to the main graphic pictured
here. Now that your layout is finished,
it's time to begin scripting in the action.

 24

There's not
much scripting to do on this three part
page. Open (Restore) the ActiveX
Control Pad with WWWolfa.htm on it.
Open the first Layout (WWWolfa.alx).
Click on the Script Wizard icon.

25

HotSpot1 is going to send you to the Microsoft Internet Explorer home page. In the Event pane (left) click on the plus (+) beside HotSpot1 and click the Click Event. In pane #2 (Insert Actions) scroll to the bottom and click on the plus(+) next to "window." Click on the plus (+) next to "location" and double-click on href. In the window.location href box type in www.microsoft.com/ie. Click OK and OK again to close the Script Wizard. Save the file and close the window.

26

Since there were no HotSpots in WWWolf2a.alx, open the third Layout (WWWolf3a.alx). Remember, the HotSpot is on the face of the wolf. Open the Script Wizard, click on the plus(+) beside HotSpot1 and select the Click Event in the left pane. In the Actions pane (right) select "window" (click +), "location" (click +), double-click "href" and enter WlfLinks.htm. Click OK in the dialog box, and OK to close the Script Wizard.

27

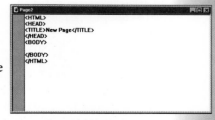

Save the Layout and the entire HTML file. Open a new HTML (File, Open New HTML) and you are ready to start with the WlfLinks.htm page.

28

Insert an HTML Layout between the body tags (Edit, Insert HTML Layout). Name it WlfLinks.alx and let the ActiveX Control Pad create it for you.

29

Open the HTML Layout to start editing. Place an Image control in the upper left corner. In the Properties window type in the new PicturePath as **C:\ CPTry5\printbak.gif** and click Apply. Change PictureSizeMode to 0-Clip and PictureTiling to -1-True. Drag the image by the lower right handle down and across to the right to fill the screen and release.

30

Place an Image control to house a horizontal bar at the top left of the screen (PicturePath, C:\CPTry5 \bar5.gif). Copy and Paste three more bars. Place another Image control between two of the bars near the top (PicturePath, C:\CPTry5\wlinks.gif).

31

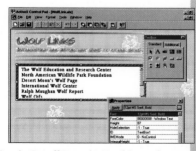

Place a TextBox control below the title and bars and change it's properties of MultiLine (1-True), ScrollBars (3-Both), and Font (MS Serif, Bold Size 12). Enter the following titles, one to a line. The Wolf Education and Research Center, North American Wildlife Park Association, Desert Moon's wolf Page, International Wolf Center, Ralph Maughan Wolf Report, Wolf Gifs, Wolf Resource Page, Wolf's Den, Wonders of the Wolf. There are a lot of other sites that can be included, but that's enough for now.

Continue to next page ▶

TRY IT!

Continue
below

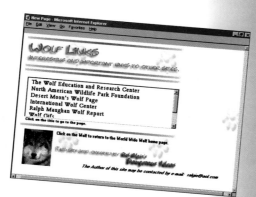

32

Surround
each of these
lines of
type with
a HotSpot
control.

33

Place another Label below the TextBox.
Make the BackStyle property 0-
Transparent, and the Caption Click on
the title to go to the page. Change the
Font Properties to MS Serif, Bold.

34

Place an Image control beneath the horizontal
bar and change the PicturePath to C:\CPTry5
\Wface2.gif. Put another HotSpot control in-
side the bounds of this Image control. Place a
Label control next to the Image of the wolf.
Change the Caption to Click on the Wolf to re-
turn to the World Wide Wolf home page. Click
Apply. Also set the BackStyle to 0-Transparent.

35

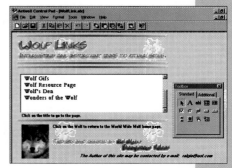

Introduce
one more
Image control
across the
bottom of the
page and set
it's Picture-
Path to C:
\CPTry5 \cre-
ated.gif. The page is now complete and
ready for scripting.

Click on the script wizard icon to open it up. We know that HotSpot10 (the last one created) is going to return us to the home page. In pane #1 click on the plus (+) next to HotSpot10 and select the Click Event. In pane #2 (Insert Actions) click on the plus (+) beside "window", click on the plus (+) beside "location", and double-click on the href icon. Type in the URL for the home page leaving off the protocol (http://), WWWolfa.htm. Click OK in the href box, but do not close the Script Wizard.

Starting with HotSpot1 repeat step 36 for each of the 9 HotSpots in the TextBox. The URLs to add are:

(1) www .wild-eyed .org/wolf1.htm,
(2)tigerden .com/Wolf-park/Welcome.html,
(3)www.scs.unr.edu/~timb/desert.html,
(4)usa.net:80/WolfHome,
(5)www.greywolf.com/rm/maughan.html,
(6)aazk.ind.net/animal-gifs/Wolves/Wolves.html,
(7)www.greywolf.com/wolf.html,
(8)www.wolfsden.org,
(9)www.halcyon.com/wolf/wolf.htm

When all the URLs are in the proper HotSpots, close the Script Wizard.

Save the WolfLink.alx Layout and close it. Click on the File menu and Save As. Save the file as WlfLinks.htm in the CPTry5 folder.

Restore Internet Explorer. If WWWolfa.htm is still on the screen, Refresh it. The connection to Microsoft wont work unless you are on a server and connected to the Internet, but you can watch your cursor change from an arrow to a cross as it passes over an active area.

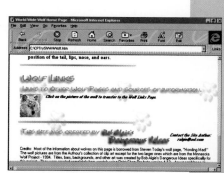

Scroll down the page and click on the picture of the wolf in the Wolf Links area to go to the other page. When you get there you may click on the wolf to return to the World Wide Wolf home page or on "Back" in the Internet Explorer toolbar.

CHAPTER 17

How to Get Your Site On the Web

 Now that you've created all those lovely Web pages, it's time to let the world see them. For this you need to use a Web server. In this chapter you will discover two ways to make your presence known on the World Wide Web: by running your own Web server or by publishing your pages on your ISP's Web server.

The Microsoft Personal Web Server turns a Windows 95-based computer into a low-volume Web server, making it easy to use your network connection to share HTML files over intranets (in the office) and the Internet. Once installed, the software is fully integrated into the Windows 95 taskbar and Control Panel allowing you to start and stop HTTP services whenever you want. Whether you want to test your new Web site or set up better intranet communications in the office, you need to have server software. The PWS is designed for small workgroups, small businesses, homes, and schools. It can be downloaded from the Microsoft Web site at **http://www.microsoft.com/ie /download/ieadd.htm**.

If you only want to upload the files in your Web site to a remote server (your ISP for instance), the Web Publishing Wizard makes it quick and easy. It can be found on the CD or downloaded at: **http://www.microsoft.com/msdownload/webpost.htm**.

Whichever way you want to go, this chapter will get you started.

How to Use the Microsoft Personal Web Server

Personal Web Server (PWS) transmits information like your Web site in Hypertext Markup Language (HTML) using the Hypertext Transport Protocol (HTTP). It has the ability to publish Web pages locally, supports Microsoft ActiveX programs, and can transmit or receive files by using the FTP service (File Transfer Protocol). In a few simple steps you can install the server software and be up and running.

 After obtaining the pws10a.exe file you can easily install the Personal Web Server by locating it with Windows Explorer and double-clicking on the file name.

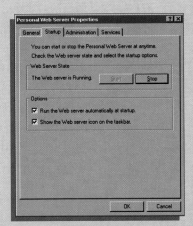

 On the Startup tab, click Start. The server is now started and your home page is located at C:\WebShare \Wwwroot\Default.htm.

2 When a dialog box appears asking you to restart your computer, click Yes. As soon as your computer has restarted, personal Web Server is installed.

3 By default your server's home directory is C:\WebShare\Wwwroot. Copy the files from the CPad17 folder into the Wwwroot folder including all .htm, .alx, and .gif files that have been created.

4 Delete Default.htm from the Wwwroot folder, then rename the Danger1.htm file to Default.htm.

5 Log in to your ISP (Internet Service Provider).

6 Click on start on the Windows taskbar, select Settings and click on Control Panel. Double-click on the Personal Web Server icon.

How to Use the Web Publishing Wizard

If your Internet Service Provider allows you to publish Web pages on their server, no doubt the simplest way to publish your site on the Web is by using the Microsoft Web Publishing Wizard. You need to know how much file space is allowed free by your provider so you don't go overboard, unless you are paying for extra space. For instance, America Online provides 2 megabytes per individual. Here's how to get the software, install it, and publish your site.

▶ **1** To install the Web Publishing Wizard from the CD double-click on the file name wp11-x86.exe. To download the Web Publishing Wizard, connect with your ISP (AOL, CompuServe, Microsoft, and so forth) and enter the URL: http://www.microsoft.com/msdownload/webpost.htm. Follow the onscreen instructions to make the download.

8 To publish, click Finish on the window that appears. You will be able to view the progress as each of your files is published. When it's completed, a message box will tell you the files have been posted successfully. Click OK.

TIP SHEET

▶ **All the various Internet Service Providers have specific locations for your Web files to go. Before using the Web Publishing Wizard you should know this information.**

▶ **If you discover you have made a mistake in your new Web site after you have loaded it with your ISP, make the correction in the ActiveX Control Pad, save the file, and use the Web Publishing Wizard to reload that file alone. When you do it will overwrite the single file. There is no need to replace all the graphics and accompanying files that are already on your site.**

7 You will then be asked to select the name of a Web server. Click on the provider you intend to use. This will also show you your URL for the site. Click Next.

2 To install the Web Publishing Wizard, double-click on the file name wp11-x86.exe. Click Yes when the End User License Agreement appears. Then when the installation is complete a message box will appear describing exactly where the Wizard is located.

3 Log into your Internet Service Provider.

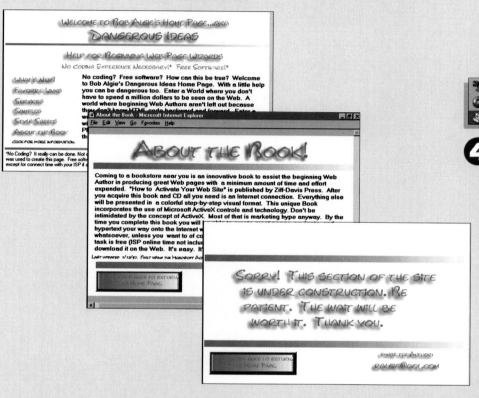

4 Once connected to your Provider, click on Start on the taskbar, and select Programs, Accessories, Internet Tools. Click on Web Publishing Wizard.

6 You will be prompted to enter the full path of the folder where all the files to your Web site are located. Either type it in or Browse to C:\CPad17\Danger. Click Next.

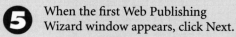

5 When the first Web Publishing Wizard window appears, click Next.

APPENDIX A

HTML Quick Reference

Even the most accomplished HTML author often needs to refer back to a listing of HTML tags when putting together complex documents. Many HTML tags support several attributes, and can be used in many different ways. Keeping all the details of HTML committed to memory is close to impossible. This reference guide is designed to help you quickly recall the HTML tags and attributes you've learned about in this book.

HTML tags are divided into sections based on tag type. For each HTML tag, a description and list of possible attributes are provided. If the HTML tag is only supported by HTML 3.2, Netscape, or Internet Explorer, that limitation is also noted. This information is taken from the HTML 3.2 draft specification, as well as the Netscape and Internet Explorer release notes. Following the listing of HTML tags is a complete reference of all the named and numbered character entities for HTML. This listing is derived from the ISO 8859/1 Latin-1 character set.

Basic Document Tags

Tag	Description	Attributes
<BASE>	Used to specify the full URL of the current document.	HREF="..."
<BODY>...</BODY>	Tag pair for the body section of the HTML document. The body section includes all of the text and markup tags in the document.	BACKGROUND="..." BGCOLOR=... TEXT=... LINK=... ALINK=... VLINK=...
<HTML>...</HTML>	Tag pair for the entire HTML document.	PROMPT="..."
<ISINDEX>	Specifies to the server that this document can be searched.	
<HEAD>...</HEAD>	Tag pair for the head section of the HTML document.	
<TITLE>...</TITLE>	Specifies the title of the document.	

Style/Formatting Tags

Tag	Description	Attributes	Support Limited to
<A>...</A>	When used with the HREF attribute, inserts a hyperlink into your HTML document. When used with the NAME attribute, inserts an anchor into your HTML document. (In HTML3, use of the <A> tag with the NAME attribute has been phased out. Instead, you should use the ID element inside block elements.)	NAME="..." HREF="..."	
<B>...</B>	Displays the enclosed characters in boldface.		
<BASEFONT>	When used with the SIZE attribute, this tag overrides the default font size for the document. The font size can be any number from 1 to 7. The default is 3.	SIZE=...	
<BIG>...</BIG>	Displays the enclosed text in a larger font.		HTML 3.2
<BLINK>...</BLINK>	Causes the enclosed text to blink repeatedly. Known to cause unpredictable behavior in laboratory animals. Use with extreme caution.		Netscape

Tag	Description	Attributes	Support Limited to
<CITE>…</CITE>	Formats the enclosed text in the logical citation style. This is used when you quote material from other works. Citation text is displayed by most browsers in italics.		
<CODE>…</CODE>	Formats the enclosed text as computer code. This is best used when you're showing examples of programming code. <CODE> text is displayed by most browsers in a monospaced font, such as Courier.		
<DFN>…</DFN>	The enclosed text is the defining instance of a term or phrase.		
<EM>…</EM>	This logical markup tag instructs the browser to display the enclosed text with emphasis. Most browsers display <EM> text in italics.		
<FONT>…</FONT>	This tag allows you to specify font attributes for the enclosed text. The <FONT> tag was originally a Netscape extension, but it is now further extended by Internet Explorer as well.	COLOR=… FACE="…" SIZE=…	
<I>…</I>	Displays the enclosed text in italics.		
<KBD>…</KBD>	This logical markup tag is used to indicate that the enclosed text should be typed in by the reader exactly as shown.		
<SAMP>…</SAMP>	This logical markup tag instructs the browser to display the enclosed text in sample style. This style is used for example material in your document.		
<SMALL>… </SMALL>	Displays the enclosed text in a smaller font.		
<STRIKE>… </STRIKE>	Displays the enclosed text in strike-through style, which places a horizontal line through the middle of the text.		
<STRONG>… </STRONG>	This logical markup tag instructs the browser to display the enclosed text with strong emphasis. Most browsers display <STRONG> text in bold.		
<SUB>…</SUB>	Displays the enclosed text in subscript, placing it slightly below the current line.		
<SUP>…</SUP>	Displays the enclosed text in superscript, placing it slightly above the current line.		

Tag	Description	Attributes	Support Limited to
<TT>...</TT>	Displays the enclosed text in typewriter style. This is displayed by most browsers in a monospaced font.		
<VAR>...</VAR>	This logical style is used to indicate variables, which are items to be supplied by the reader of the document.		

Block Elements

Tag	Description	Attributes	Support Limited to
<ADDRESS>... </ADDRESS>	The enclosed text is defined as specific address information, and is often used to indicate such information as e-mail address, signature, or authorship of the document. The <ADDRESS> information usually appears at the very top or bottom of the HTML document. Most browsers display <ADDRESS> information in italics. The address element implies a paragraph break before and after.		
<BLOCKQUOTE>... </BLOCKQUOTE>	Used to mark a section (block) of text as a quote from another source. <BLOCKQUOTE> text is indented and spaced apart from the current paragraph by most browsers.		
 ...</BR>	Inserts a line break at a specific point in the document.		
<CENTER>... </CENTER>	Everything between these tags is centered in the document.		
<H1>...</H1>	Creates a headline. The number following the H can have a value from 1 to 6, with 1 creating the largest headline.	ALIGN=...	
<HR>...</HR>	Places a horizontal rule across the document.	NOSHADE SIZE=... WIDTH=...	

Tag	Description	Attributes	Support Limited to
<MARQUEE>... </MARQUEE>	Inserts a scrolling text marquee in the document.	BEHAVIOR=... BGCOLOR=... DIRECTION=... HEIGHT=... LOOP=... SCROLLAMOUNT=... SCROLLDELAY=... WIDTH=...	Internet Explorer
<P>...</P>	Places a paragraph inside the document. The closing </P> tag is optional, but highly recommended, especially with HTML 3.2.	ALIGN=... ID="..."	
<PRE>...</PRE>	The enclosed text is preformatted. It is displayed in a monospaced font exactly as it appears in the HTML source code.		

Form Elements

Tag	Description	Attributes	Support Limited to
<FORM>... </FORM>	Inserts an input form into the HTML document. Used to define an area containing input fields for user feedback. The two attributes, ACTION and METHOD, are required.	ACTION=... METHOD=...	
<INPUT>	Inserts an input field in the form. The type of input field is determined using the TYPE attribute. Acceptable values for TYPE are TEXT, CHECKBOX, RADIO, SUBMIT, RESET, and HIDDEN.	CHECKED MAXLENGTH=... NAME=... SIZE=... TYPE=... VALUE=...	
<OPTION>... </OPTION>	Defines an item for a SELECT input object.	SELECTED	
<SELECT>... </SELECT>	Inserts a selection input object, pop-up menu.	MULTIPLE NAME=... SIZE=...	
<TEXTAREA>... </TEXTAREA>	Inserts a multiline text input field.	COLS=... NAME=... ROWS=...	

Hypertext Link Elements

Tag	Description	Attributes	Support Limited to
<A>...</A>	Marks the beginning and end of a hypertext link. Also used by earlier versions of HTML to mark an anchor by using the NAME attribute. Although still supported by HTML3, this use of the <A> and </A> tag pair has been superseded by the ID attribute.	HREF=... NAME=...	
<AREA>	Defines a clickable region inside a client-side image map.	COORDS=x,y,x,y HREF=... NOHREF SHAPE=...	
<MAP>...</MAP>	Defines a client-side image map.	NAME=...	

Image and Sound Tags

Tag	Description	Attributes	Support Limited to
<BGSOUND>	Instructs the browser to play a sound or music file (.WAV or MIDI format) in the background.	LOOP=... SRC="..."	Internet Explorer
<IMG>	Inserts an inline image into the HTML document.	ALIGN=... ALT="..." BORDER=... CONTROLS DYNSRC="..." HEIGHT=... HSPACE=... ISMAP LOOP=... SRC="..." START=... USEMAP VSPACE=... WIDTH=...	

List Elements

Tag	Description	Attributes
<DD>…</DD>	Inserts a definition description into a <DL> definition list. Used in conjunction with a <DT>…</DT> tag pair.	
<DL>…</DL>	Inserts a definition list into the HTML document. Use the <DD> and <DT> tags to insert list items.	
<DT>…</DT>	Inserts a definition title into a <DL> definition list. Used in conjunction with a <DD>…</DD> tag pair.	
<LI>…</LI>	List item. Used with both ordered and unordered lists. The closing </LI> tag is optional.	
<OL>…</OL>	Ordered list. Creates a list with items presented in sequential order.	SEQNUM=… TYPE=… CONTINUE
<UL>…</UL>	Unordered list. Creates a bulleted list of items presented in no particular order.	TYPE=…

Table Elements

Tag	Description	Attributes
<CAPTION>… </CAPTION>	Inserts a caption for the table.	ALIGN=…
<TABLE>… </TABLE>	Inserts a table in the HTML document.	BGCOLOR=… BORDER=… BORDERCOLOR=… BORDERCOLORDARK=… BORDERCOLORLIGHT=… WIDTH=… CELLSPACING=… CELLPADDING=…
<TD>…</TD>	Inserts a table data cell.	BGCOLOR=… ROWSPAN=… COLSPAN=… ALIGN=… VALIGN=…
<TH>…</TH>	Inserts a table header cell. The text contained inside is usually displayed in bold and is centered inside the cell.	BGCOLOR=… ROWSPAN=… COLSPAN=… ALIGN=… VALIGN=…

Tag	Description	Attributes
<TR>...</TR>	Defines a table row. All of the <TD>.and <TH> tags enclosed will appear in the same row of the table.	ALIGN=... BGCOLOR=... VALIGN=...

Character Entities

Commonly Used Characters

Entity	Description	Example
&copy;	copyright symbol	©
&reg;	registered trademark symbol	®
&#153;	trademark symbol	™
	nonbreaking space	
&lt;	less-than symbol	<
&gt;	greater-than symbol	>
&amp;	ampersand	&
&quot;	quotation mark	"

Latin 1 Character Set (Named Character Entities)

This list is derived from the ISO 8859/1 character set. All of the entity names are case-sensitive.

Entity	Description	Example
&Aacute;	Capital A, acute accent	Á
&Agrave;	Capital A, grave accent	À
&Acirc;	Capital A, circumflex accent	Â
&Atilde;	Capital A, tilde	Ã
&Aring;	Capital A, ring	Å
&Auml;	Capital A, dieresis or umlaut mark	Ä
&AElig;	Capital AE dipthong (ligature)	Æ
&Ccedil;	Capital C, cedilla	Ç
&Eacute;	Capital E, acute accent	É
&Egrave;	Capital E, grave accent	È
&Ecirc;	Capital E, circumflex accent	Ê
&Euml;	Capital E, dieresis or umlaut mark	Ë

Entity	Description	Example
Í	Capital I, acute accent	Í
Ì	Capital I, grave accent	Ì
Î	Capital I, circumflex accent	Î
Ï	Capital I, dieresis or umlaut mark	Ï
Ð	Capital Eth, Icelandic	
Ñ	Capital N, tilde	Ñ
Ó	Capital O, acute accent	Ó
Ò	Capital O, grave accent	Ò
Ô	Capital O, circumflex accent	Ô
Õ	Capital O, tilde	Õ
Ö	Capital O, dieresis or umlaut mark	Ö
&Oslash	Capital O, slash	Ø
Ú	Capital U, acute accent	Ú
Ù	Capital U, grave accent	Ù
Û	Capital U, circumflex accent	Û
Ü	Capital U, dieresis or umlaut mark	Ü
Ý	Capital Y, acute accent	Ý
Þ	Capital THORN, Icelandic	
á	Small a, acute accent	á
à	Small a, grave accent	à
â	Small a, circumflex accent	â
ã	Small a, tilde	ã
ä	Small a, dieresis or umlaut mark	ä
æ	Small ae dipthong (ligature)	æ
ç	Small c, cedilla	ç
é	Small e, acute accent	é
è	Small e, grave accent	è
ê	Small e, circumflex accent	ê
ë	Small e, dieresis or umlaut mark	ë
í	Small i, acute accent	í
ì	Small i, grave accent	ì
î	Small i, circumflex accent	î
ï	Small i, dieresis or umlaut mark	ï
ð	Small eth, Icelandic	∂

Entity	Description	Example
&ntilde	Small n, tilde	ñ
ó	Small o, acute accent	ó
ò	Small o, grave accent	ò
ô	Small o, circumflex accent	ô
õ	Small o, tilde	õ
ö	Small o, dieresis or umlaut mark	ö
&oslash	Small o, slash	ø
ß	Small sharp s, German (sz ligature)	ß
&uacute	Small u, acute accent	ú
&ugrave	Small u, grave accent	ù
û	Small u, circumflex accent	û
ü	Small u, dieresis or umlaut mark	ü
&yacute	Small y, acute accent	ý
þ	Small thorn, Icelandic	
ÿ	Small y, dieresis or umlaut mark	ÿ

Numbered Character Entities

Entity	Description	Example
&#01; - &#08;	Unused	
		Horizontal tab	

	Line feed	

&#11; - &#31;	Unused	
 	Space	
!	Exclamation mark	!
"	Quotation mark	"
#	Number sign	#
$	Dollar sign	$
%	Percent sign	%
&	Ampersand	&
'	Apostrophe	'
(	Left parenthesis	(
)	Right parenthesis	)
*	Asterisk	*
+	Plus sign	+

Entity	Description	Example
&#44;	Comma	,
&#45;	Hyphen	-
&#46;	Period	.
&#47;	Forward slash	/
0 - 9	Digits 0–9	
&#58;	Colon	:
&#59;	Semicolon	;
&#60;	Less-than symbol	<
&#61;	Equal sign	=
&#62;	Greater-than symbol	>
&#63;	Question mark	?
&#64;	Commercial at	@
A - Z	Letters A–Z	
&#91;	Left square bracket	[
&#92;	Reverse solidus (backslash)	\
&#93;	Right square bracket	]
&#94;	Circumflex	^
&#95;	Horizontal bar	_
&#96;	Grave accent	`
a - z	Letters a–z	
&#123;	Left curly brace	{
|	Vertical bar		
&#125;	Right curly brace	}
&#126;	Tilde	~
&#127; -	Unused	
&#161;	Inverted exclamation	¡
&#162;	Cent sign	¢
&#163;	Pound sterling	£
&#164;	General currency sign	¤
&#165;	Yen sign	¥
&#166;	Broken vertical bar (pipe symbol)		
&#167;	Section sign	§
&#168;	Umlaut (dieresis)	¨
&#169;	Copyright	©

Entity	Description	Example
ª	Feminine ordinal	a
«	Left angle quote, guillemotleft	«
¬	Not sign	¬
­	Soft hyphen	−
®	Registered trademark	®
¯	Macron accent	‾
°	Degree sign	°
±	Plus or minus	±
²	Superscript two	2
³	Superscript three	3
´	Acute accent	´
µ	Micro sign	μ
¶	Paragraph sign	¶
·	Middle dot	·
¸	Cedilla	¸
¹	Superscript one	1
º	Masculine ordinal	o
»	Right angle quote, guillemotright	»
¼	Fraction one-fourth	¼
½	Fraction one-half	½
¾	Fraction three-fourths	¾
¿	Inverted question mark	¿
À	Capital A, grave accent	À
Á	Capital A, acute accent	Á
Â	Capital A, circumflex accent	Â
Ã	Capital A, tilde	Ã
Ä	Capital A, ring	Å
Å	Capital A, dieresis or umlaut mark	Ä
Æ	Capital AE dipthong (ligature)	Æ
Ç	Capital C, cedilla	Ç
È	Capital E, grave accent	È
É	Capital E, acute accent	É
Ê	Capital E, circumflex accent	Ê
Ë	Capital E, dieresis or umlaut mark	Ë

Entity	Description	Example
Ì	Capital I, grave accent	Ì
Í	Capital I, acute accent	Í
Î	Capital I, circumflex accent	Î
Ï	Capital I, dieresis or umlaut mark	Ï
Ð	Capital Eth, Icelandic	
Ñ	Capital N, tilde	Ñ
Ò	Capital O, grave accent	Ò
Ó	Capital O, acute accent	Ó
Ô	Capital O, circumflex accent	Ô
Õ	Capital O, tilde	Õ
Ö	Capital O, dieresis or umlaut mark	Ö
×	Multiplication sign	x
Ø	Capital O, slash	Ø
Ù	Capital U, grave accent	Ù
Ú	Capital U, acute accent	Ú
Û	Capital U, circumflex accent	Û
Ü	Capital U, dieresis or umlaut mark	Ü
Ý	Capital Y, acute accent	Ý
Þ	Capital THORN, Icelandic	
ß	Small sharp s, German (sz ligature)	ß
à	Small a, grave accent	à
á	Small a, acute accent	á
â	Small a, circumflex accent	â
ã	Small a, tilde	ã
ä	Small a, ring	å
å	Small a, dieresis or umlaut mark	ä
æ	Small ae dipthong (ligature)	æ
ç	Small c, cedilla	ç
è	Small e, grave accent	è
é	Small e, acute accent	é
ê	Small e, circumflex accent	ê
ë	Small e, dieresis or umlaut mark	ë
ì	Small i, grave accent	ì
í	Small i, acute accent	í

Entity	Description	Example
î	Small i, circumflex accent	î
ï	Small i, dieresis or umlaut mark	ï
ð	Small eth, Icelandic	∂
ñ	Small n, tilde	ñ
ò	Small o, grave accent	ò
ó	Small o, acute accent	ó
ô	Small o, circumflex accent	ô
õ	Small o, tilde	õ
ö	Small o, dieresis or umlaut mark	ö
÷	Division sign	÷
ø	Small o, slash	ø
ù	Small u, grave accent	ù
ú	Small u, acute accent	ú
û	Small u, circumflex accent	û
ü	Small u, dieresis or umlaut mark	ü
ý	Small y, acute accent	ý
þ	Small thorn, Icelandic	
ÿ	Small y, dieresis or umlaut mark	ÿ

APPENDIX B

What's On the CD

 The CD-ROM included with this book contains all the necessary software you need to build a first class Web site. The contents of the CD are divided into two areas: software and chapters. This appendix gives you a brief overview of the contents of the CD. For a more detailed look at these resources, load the CD-ROM and browse the contents.

Other than the software provided with the CD all you will need to publish your Web documents is an Internet Service Provider (ISP).

Software

MICROSOFT ACTIVEX CONTROL PAD

This is the main tool used throughout this book to construct Web pages and Web sites.

Web Location: http://www.microsoft.com/workshop/author/cpad

MICROSOFT INTERNET EXPLORER 3.0

A premium Web browser and the best platform to use for viewing work in progress.

Web Location: http://www.microsoft.com/ie

Chapters

Throughout this book you are asked to download folders to use while performing the various tasks and exercises. The folder titles either begins with Cpad*number* (like CPad13 for Chapter 13) or CPTry*number* (CPTry4 for instance for the Try It section 4). The CP or CPad designation stands for ActiveX Control Pad. Here is a brief overview of what you will find in the chapters. The README.txt file in each chapter gives a little deeper explanation.

CPad1: Organization and installation of necessary software.

CPad2: The ActiveX Control Pad and its features.

CPad3: Your hardware and the launching of Internet Explorer and ActiveX Control Pad.

Cpad4: Planning and developing a useful Web site. HTML by example.

CPad5: Creating and viewing your first Web page.

Cpad6: Adding ActiveX controls and their properties.

CPad7: Using the Script Wizard to add actions to ActiveX controls.

CPTry1: Try what you have learned so far.

CPad8: Use of the versatile HTML Layout control, enhancing control images, and how to apply hypertext activities.

CPad9: Frames, framesets, and floating frames.

CPTry2: Try out your skills.

CPad10: Images, backgrounds, and rules.

CPTry3: Try out your new skills.

CPad11: Buttons, Button Bars, Dropped Shadows, Muted and Embossed Backgrounds (Paint Shop Pro needed for this chapter).

CPad12: Designing an eye-catching Web site and making graphics fit.

CPad13: Using HTML templates and creating template areas.

CPad14: Creating HTML templates.

CPTry4: Try out what you have learned.

CPad15: Creating and using the TabStrip control.

CPad16: Creating HTML tables.

CPTry5: Try your skills to build a complete Web site.

CPad17: Getting your site on the Web.

Additional Software not Included on the CD

Although not required for the creation of a Web site, below are additional software titles you may want to consider. The software manufacturers and their URLs are listed below, or you can link directly through the author's Web site, **http://members.aol.com/ralgie/danger1.htm.**

MICROSOFT INTERNET EXPLORER MULTIMEDIA GALLERY

A group of "theme" backgrounds, horizontal rules, buttons, sounds, and video that are coordinated for Web page cohesiveness. Use these graphics and you can't go wrong for a good look and feel to your Web pages.

Web Location: http://www.microsoft.com/workshop/design /mmgallry

MICROSOFT PERSONAL WEB SERVER

A good low volume server for use on intranets and small operations. A good way to test a Web site before putting it on the Web.

Web Location: http://www.microsoft.com/msdownload

MICROSOFT WEB PUBLISHING WIZARD

This makes it easy to post Web pages on the Internet. It automates the process of copying files from your computer to the Web server. It can post to local ISPs, CompuServe, America Online, and Internet servers on your Local Area Network.

Web Location: http://www.microsoft.com/msdownload

ACTIVEX PLUG-IN FOR NETSCAPE

Allows ActiveX support for Netscape Navigator 2.0 and up.

Web Location: http://www.ncompasslabs.com

PAINT SHOP PRO

Complete Windows graphics program for image creation, viewing and manipulation. Shareware version available. PSP was used extensively throughout this book and on the author's Web site.

Web Location: http://www.jasc.com

MICROSOFT IMAGE COMPOSER

A great tool for creation and manipulation of Web graphics. Included in FrontPage 97.

Web Location: http://www.microsoft.com/imagecomposer

MCAFEE ANTIVIRUS

Antivirus protection for Windows and DOS is a necessity when constantly moving files from place to place.

Web Location: http://www.mcafee.com

WINZIP

Necessary file compression utility when dealing with lots of images and pages.

Web Location: http://www.winzip.com/winzip

NETCARTA WEBMAPPER TRIAL VERSION

An excellent program for mapping, it can be used as a sort of debugger for Web sites. It points out all the lost or non-functional links.

Web Location: http://www.netcarta.com

ICAT TRIAL VERSION

Build product catalogs for the Internet. Trial version limits the number of items. If you are interested in Internet commerce, this is for you.

Web Location: http://www.icat.com

CREDITS

We would like to thank the following individuals and companies whose content appears in *How to Activate Your Web Site.*

Royal Gorge Cross Country Ski Resort

JASC (JASC home page, http://www.jasc.com)

Kate Hutchinson (NetCarta home page, http://www.netcarta.com)

MECC (MECC home page, http://www.mecc.com)

Karawynn Long (RAINFROG web site, http://www.rainfrog.com)

Tom & Ray Magliozzi (Car Talk web site, http://www.cartalk.com)

Electronic Arts (EA Web site, http://www.ea.com)

Velo News (Velo News Web site, http://www.velonews.com)

INDEX